I0502506

The Art and Studio of Jorge Leyva – Paintings and Sculptures by the Artist

By Robert H. Scott, Jr.

Copyright 2013, All Rights Reserved

All images in this book have been provided by the artist, Jorge Leyva, and remain his property. Reproduction in this book is by his permission and may not be reproduced further without his permission

INTRODUCTION TO THE ARTIST

With his studio in the heart of the Ozark Mountains Jorge Leyva has brought an unusual talent to his paintings and sculptures that has attracted collectors around the country and indeed around the world. His unique style of modern impressionism has found a place in the hearts and collections of those who appreciate his style. His wide ranging art hangs in public galleries as well as private residences and businesses. In his paintings his focus is on nature scenes but in a way very different from other artists. The description of his focus on nature is expressed in his note on the Nüart gallery website showing his work in Santa Fe, New Mexico where the interested reader can see a great deal more of his art than in this volume which is devoted to introducing the reader to the artist.
http://www.nuartgallery.com/artists/jorge-leyva/

"unlike legible written language that we can understand, nature's language is produced by muted sounds, which is the process of creative thought."

Born in Peru in 1958 he came to this country at an early age to Joplin, Missouri. He graduated from Missouri Southern State University with a BA in art and was a member of the Dean's honor roll and president of the Art League. He went on to Pittsburg State University for a MA in art. A member of Phi Kappa Phi national honor society he went on to receive a Master of Fine Arts (MFA) degree from the California College of the Arts in 1993 where he was a member of the President's Circle. In 2005-2006 he was recognized in Strathmore's Who's Who.

His art hangs in numerous galleries, including Spiva Center for the Arts in Joplin, Missouri, the Daum Museum of Contemporary Art, Sedalia, Missouri, the Birger Sandzen Memorial Gallery, Lindsborg, Kansas and the Nüart Gallery in Santa Fe, New Mexico.

Examples of his art can be found at both the Nüart Gallery website and his artist's website.
http://www.jorgeleyvastudio.com/

THE STUDIO OF JORGE LEYVA

Located in a tranquil setting in the Ozarks where the artist and visitors can contemplate nature his studio comprises of a large painting room, a sculpture room and a variety of other spaces devoted to both producing and showing his art.

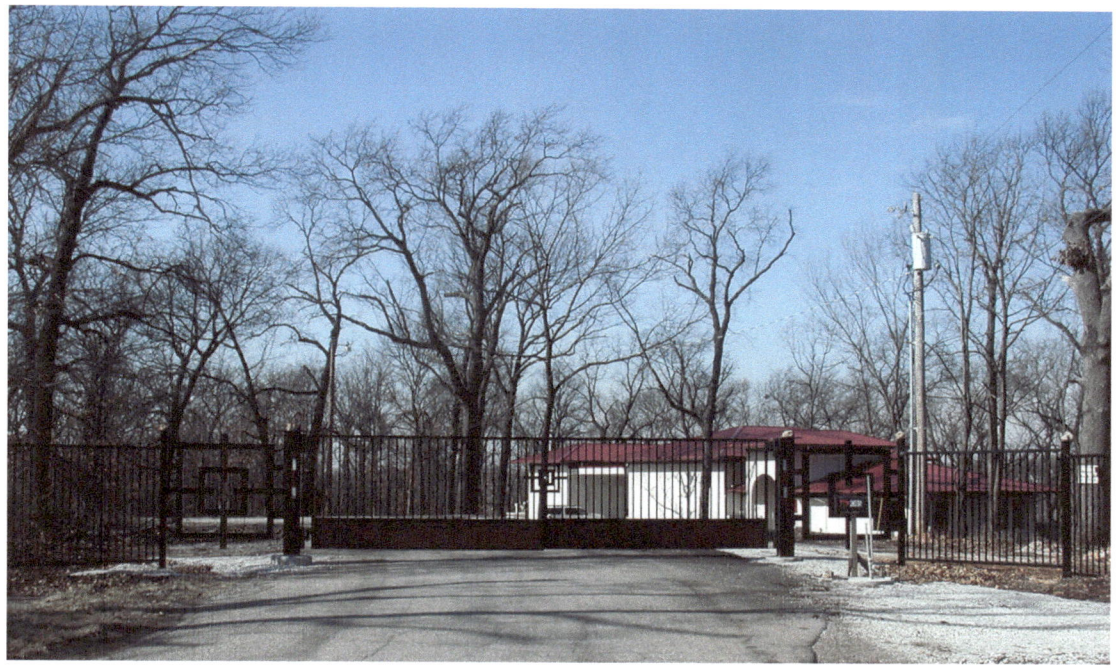

View from Vandalia Stret of entrance to the studio

The painting room is large enough to look out over a wooded area while providing storage and work area for the artist and ample room for display of both oil painting and sculpture. Annually the artist invites other artists to his studio for an open house displaying their works. A generous talent willing to share both his time and talent with others Jorge is open to both other artists and visitors interested in his work.

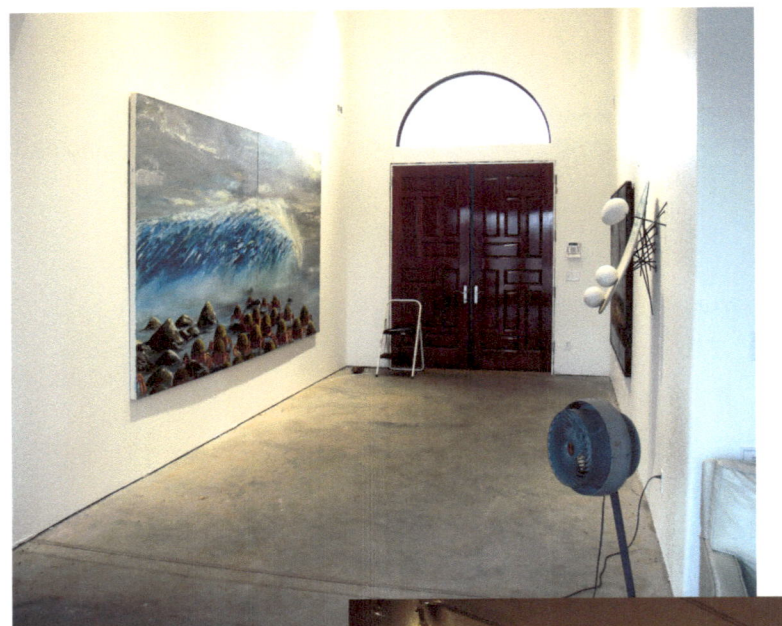

Entrance hall to the studio

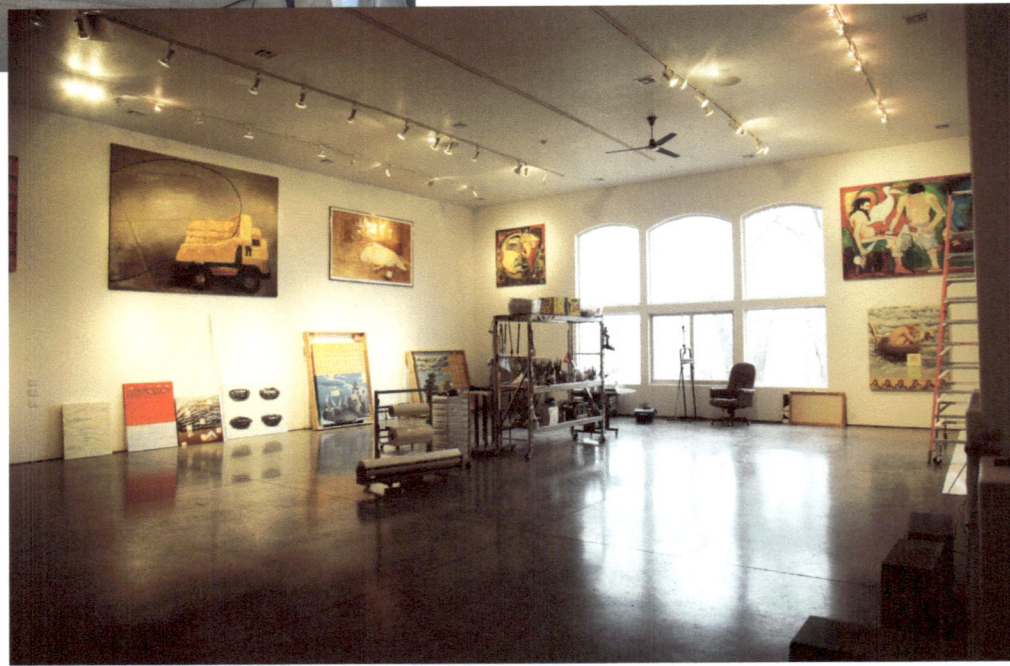

The Painting Room

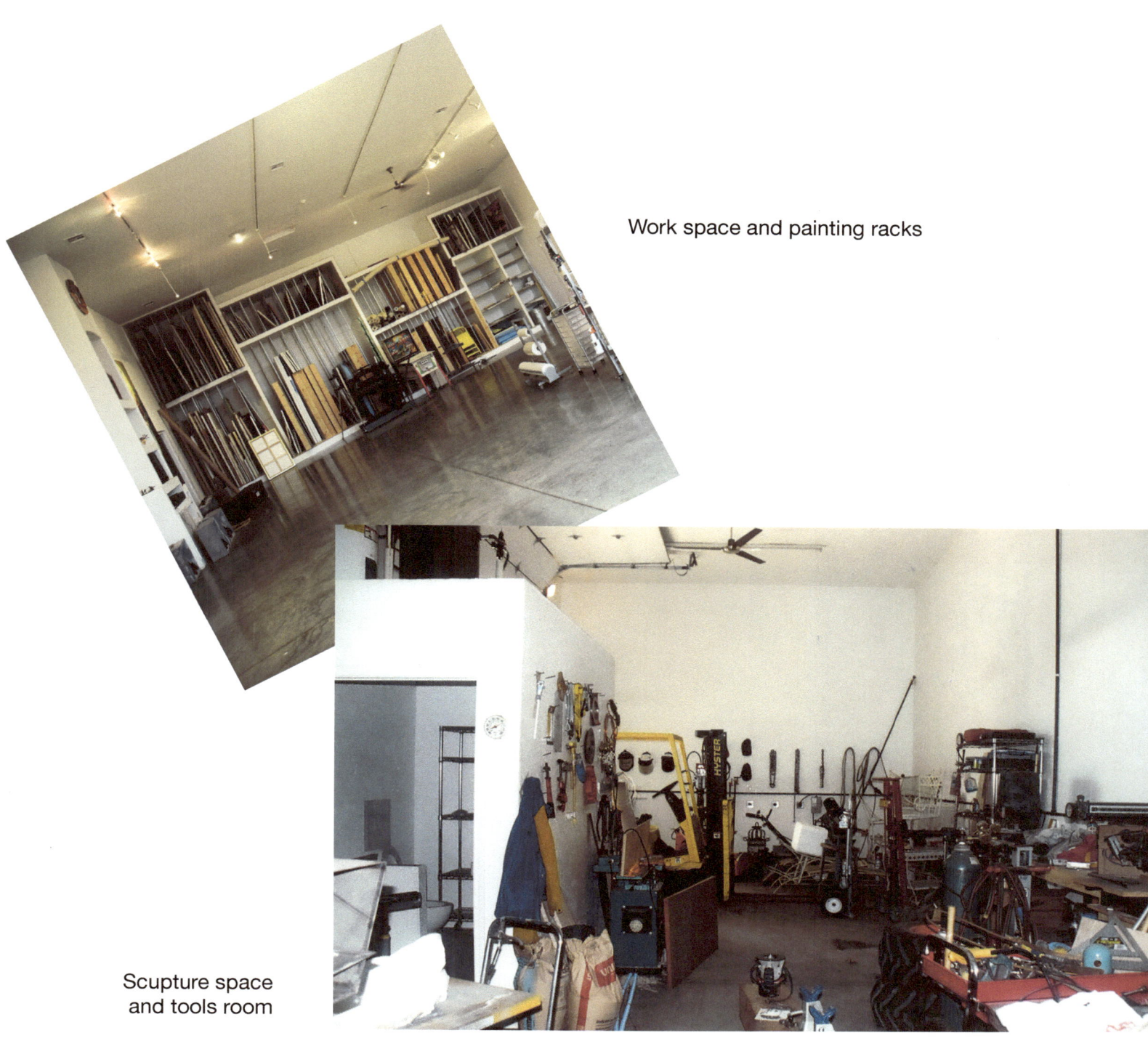

Work space and painting racks

Scupture space
and tools room

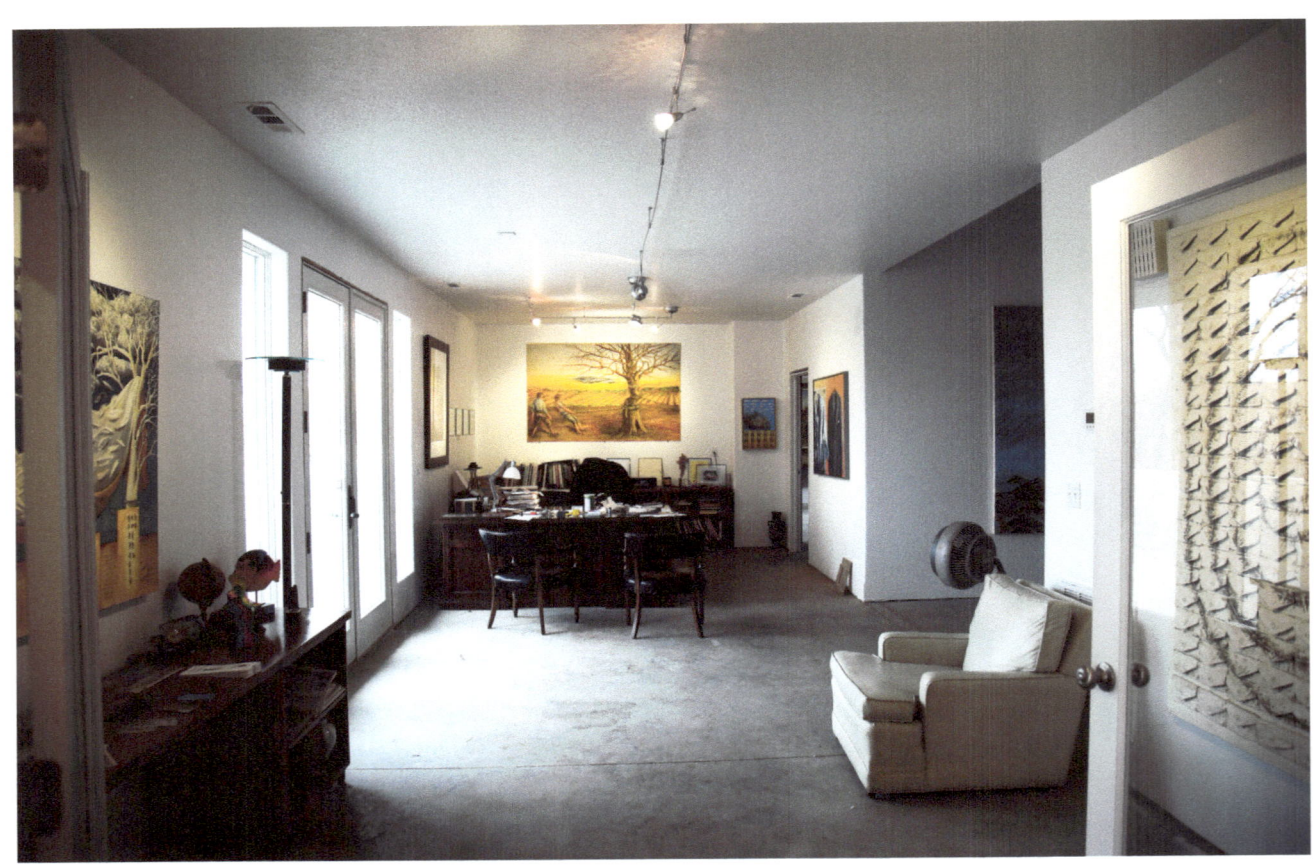

The artist's office

Always with time to spend with young artists and with those interested in his art his airy studio is both friendly as well as professional atmosphere.

INTRODUCTION TO THE ART OF JORGE LEYVA

As the images in this book show, Jorge Leyva has displayed over his many years as a professional artist a unique range of interest both in paintings and sculpture using a variety of media and styles. He is not afraid to mix media and styles or to challenge the artistic viewer with images that call for thoughtful contemplation. In his paintings in recent years his focus has been on nature and architectural forms expressing it in a unique contemporary style that is both interesting and thought provoking.

While he has done representational art in the form of murals, his general style has been one to produce in the lover of art a different way of looking at both art and the subjects of his art.

In Volume I of his art the author has sought to show the range of Jorge Leyva's talents from mural size oil paintings to more modest sizes for home or office as well as major sculpture pieces in a variety of materials.

In his own words Jorge says that, "The evolution of my paintings continues to find and explore the endless possibilities of surface materials and media. The persistent constant that challenges my work is the content, which allows me to develop a philosophy. From figurative paintings with metaphors for life, to the cultural influences of a rich and colorful background, my paintings today are becoming dramatically universal. I like to think of my work as being the result of the present; it is the awareness of my everyday growth as an artist and a reflection of my responsibility to the natural things that I love. The nests and creatures are the subjects that afford me the freedom to express my curiosity about nature. The restricting devises and the non-descriptive language reflects the angst of a society incapable of freeing and preserving the gifts granted us by a creative nature."

The best way to understand Jorge Leyva and his art is not through the author or even the artist's description of his work but rather to let the reader experience his art in visual form. The remainder of this book will show the range and power of his talent from his earliest days as a professional artist to his current work.

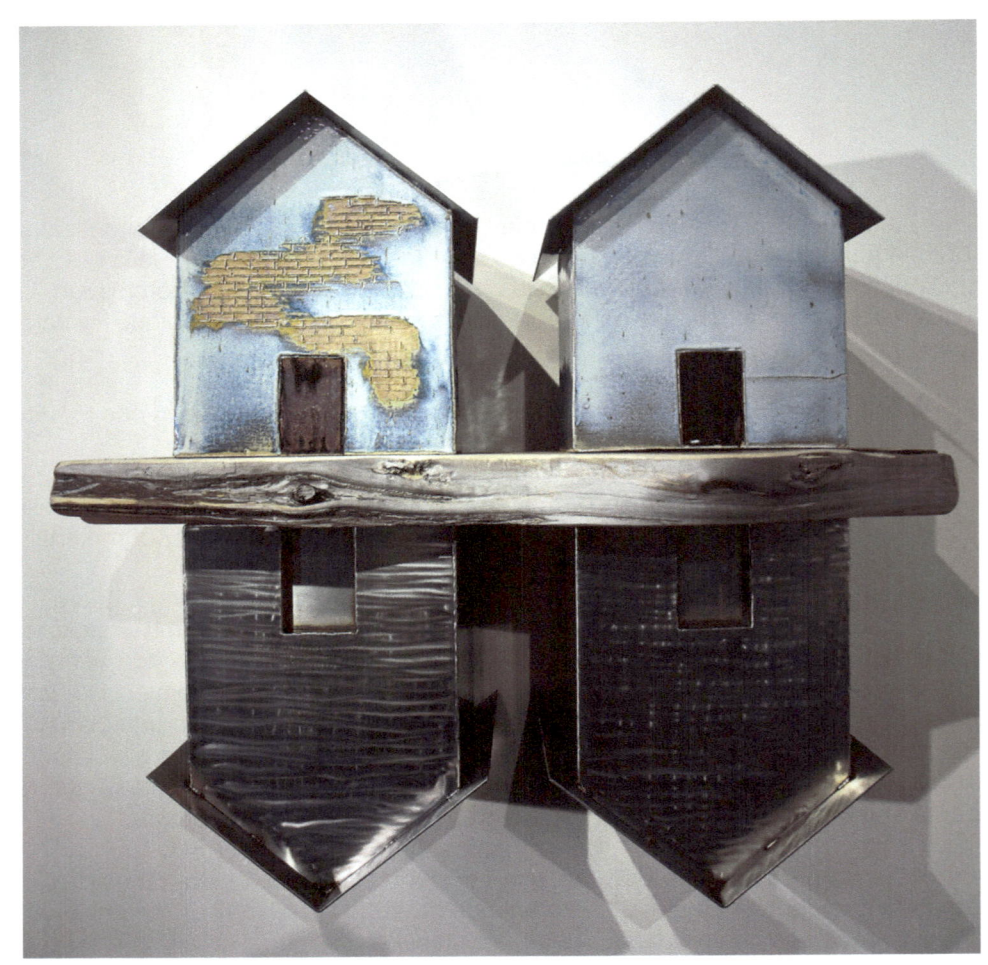

Calm Shores of Summer Still, clay, stainless steel, wood   2013

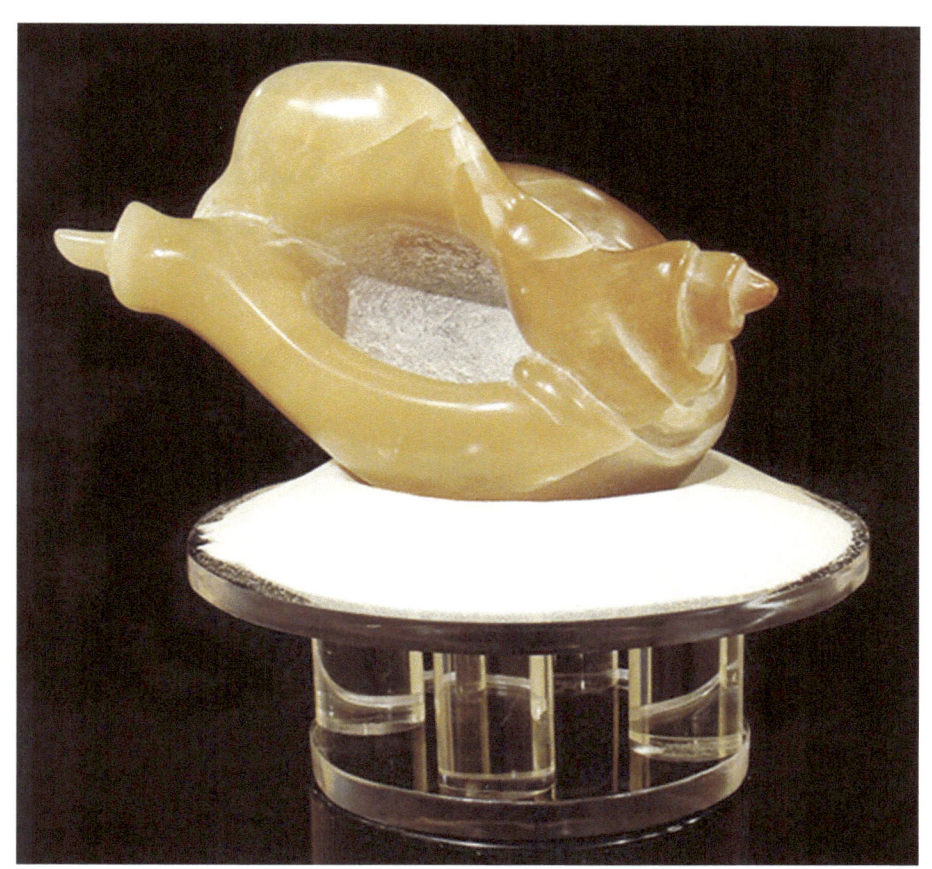

Conch, orange calcite   2006

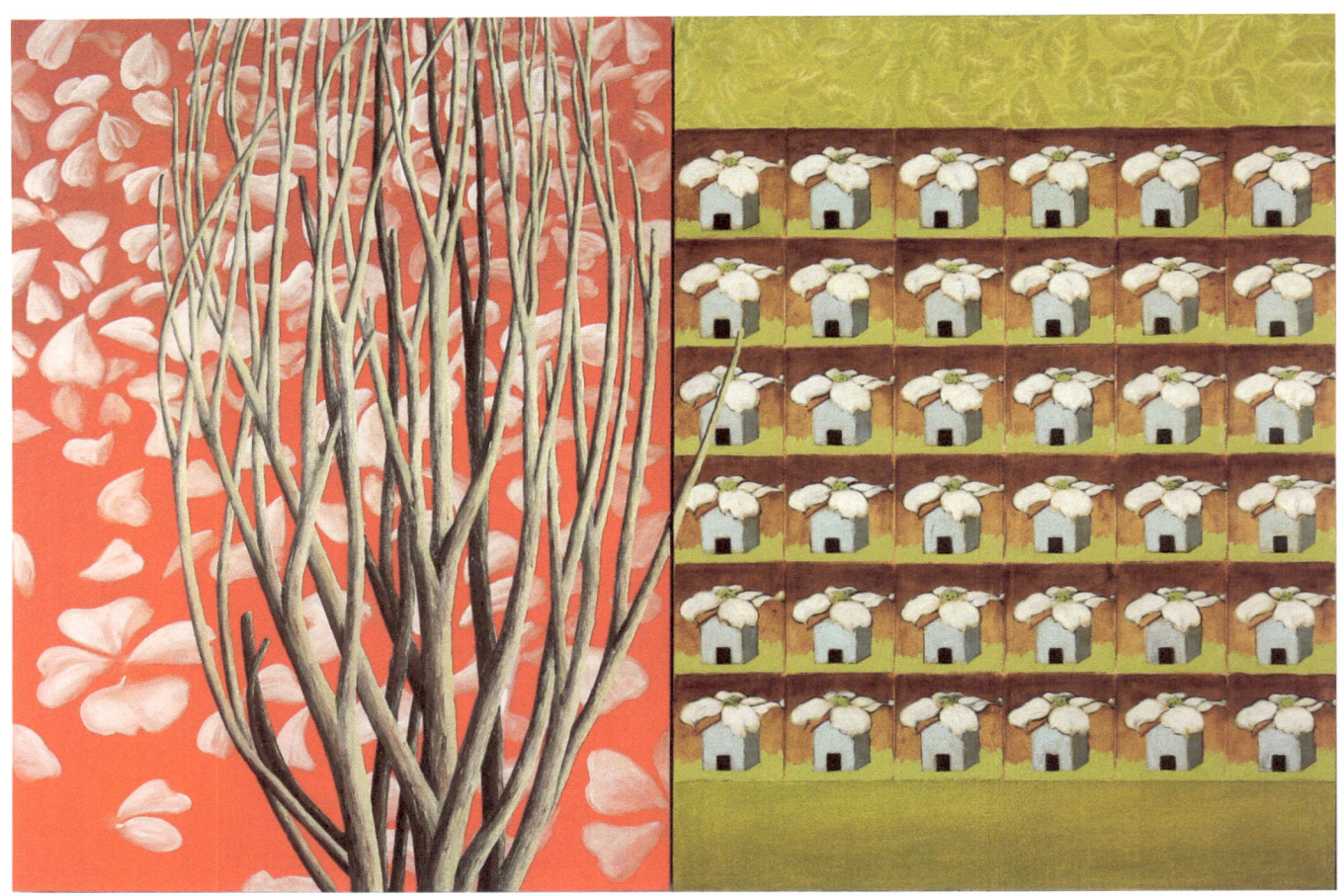

Dogwood Houses, oil on panel   2013

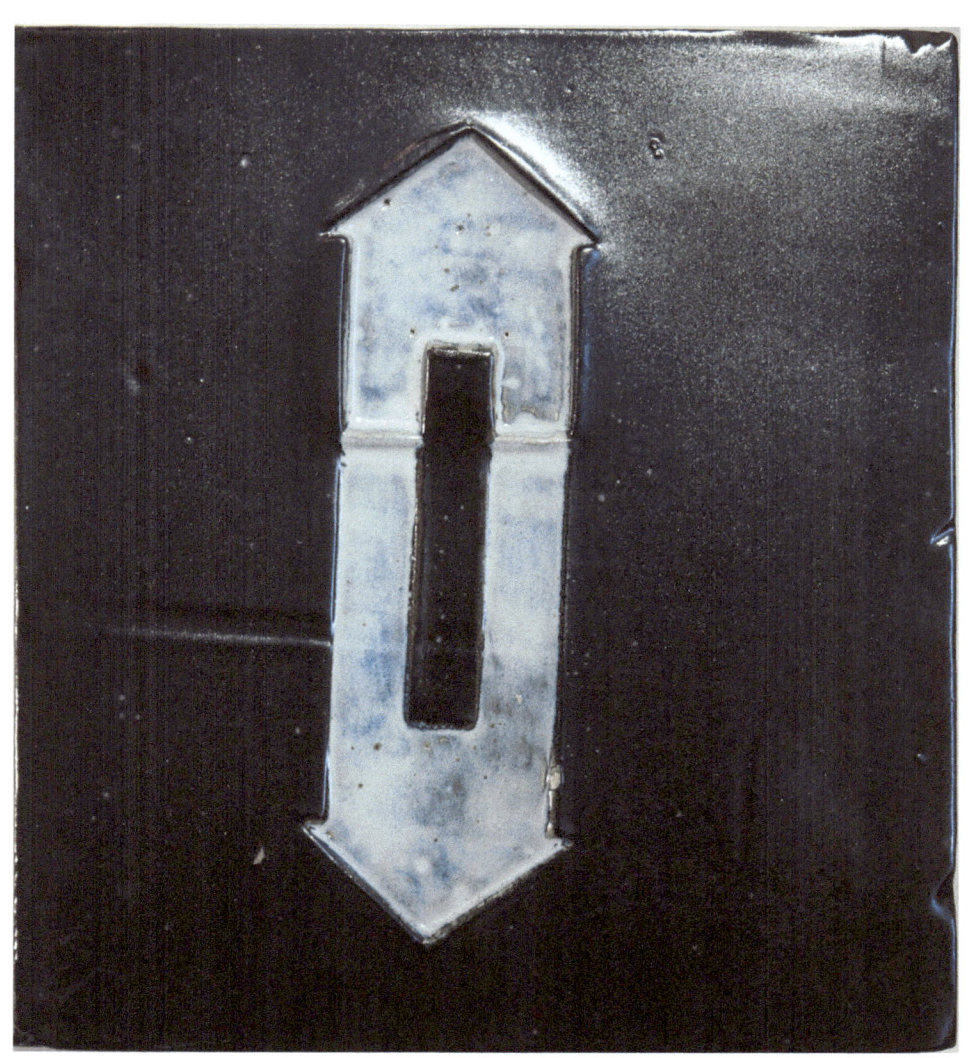

Evening Reflection, glazed clay   2013

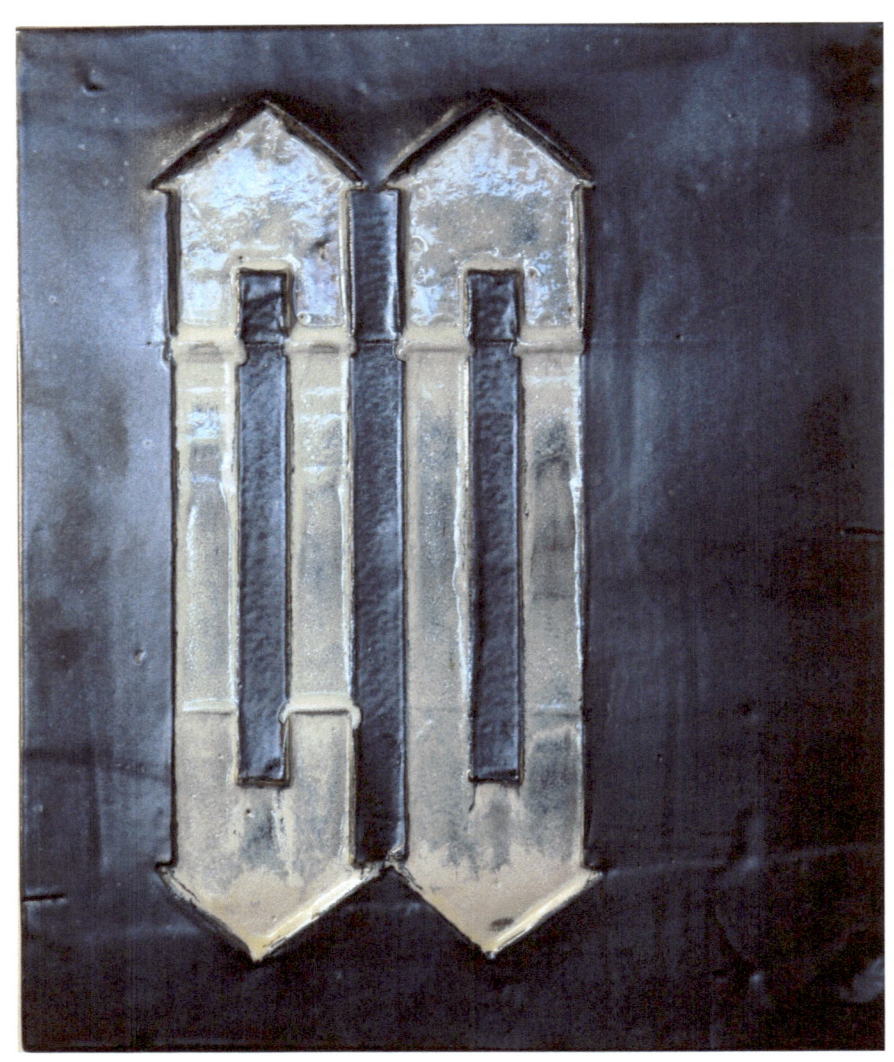

Evening Reflections, glazed clay   2013

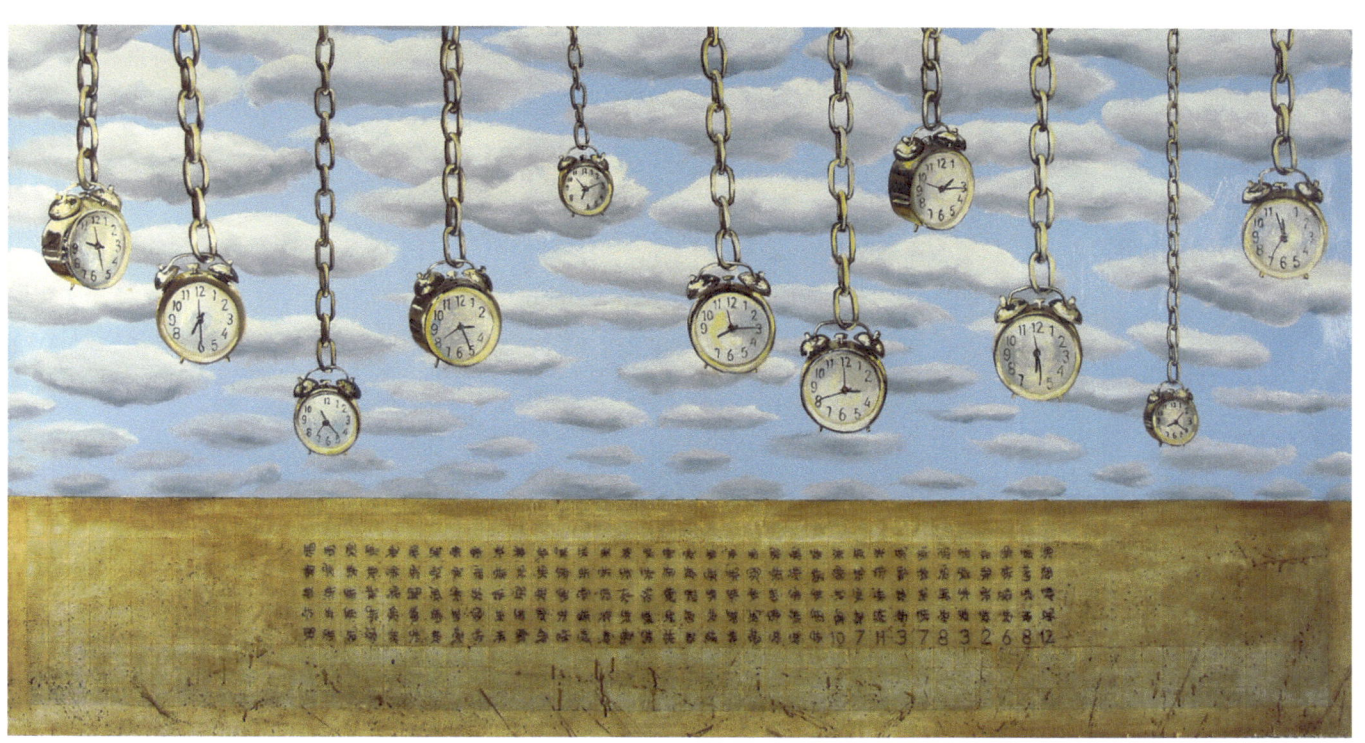

Field of Hours, oil, wax, on primed paper   2001

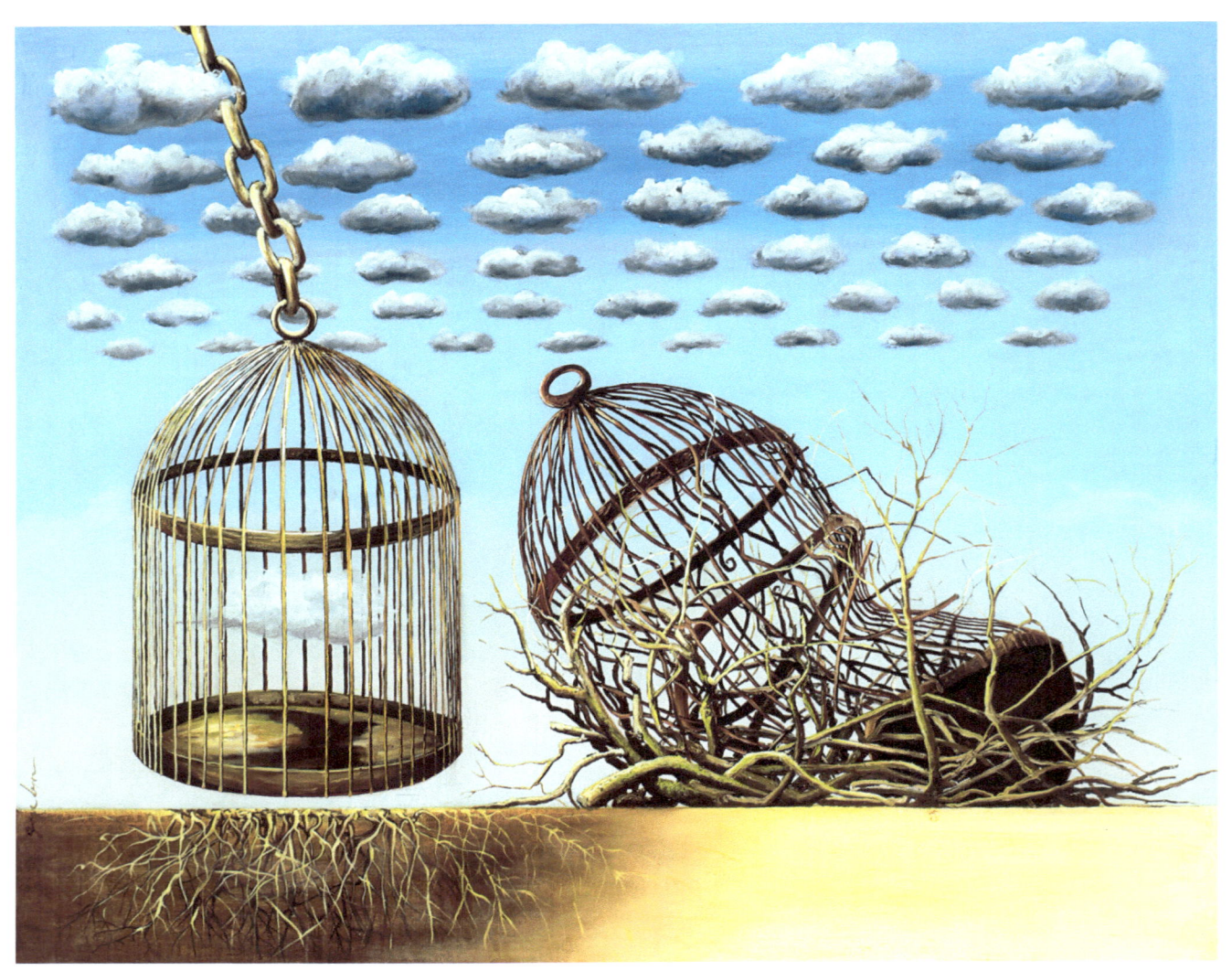

Handmade Nature, oil on panel   2005

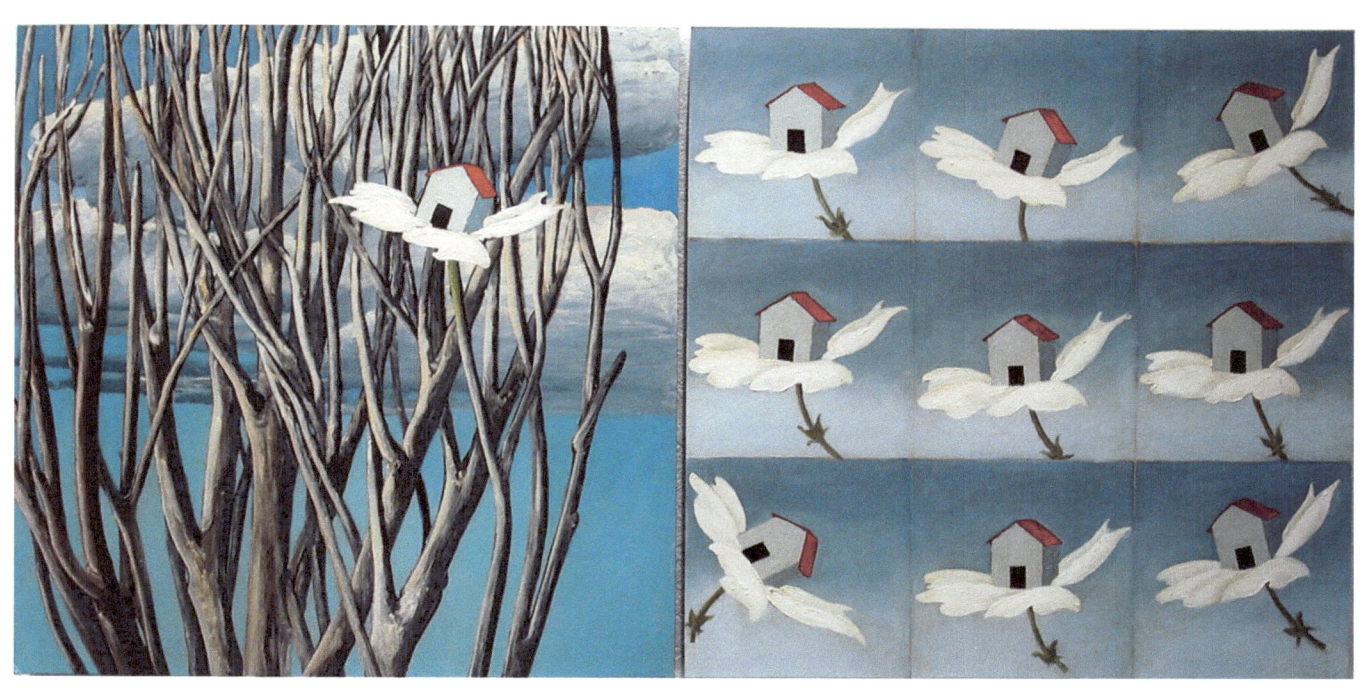

Into the Dogwood, oil on panel 2012

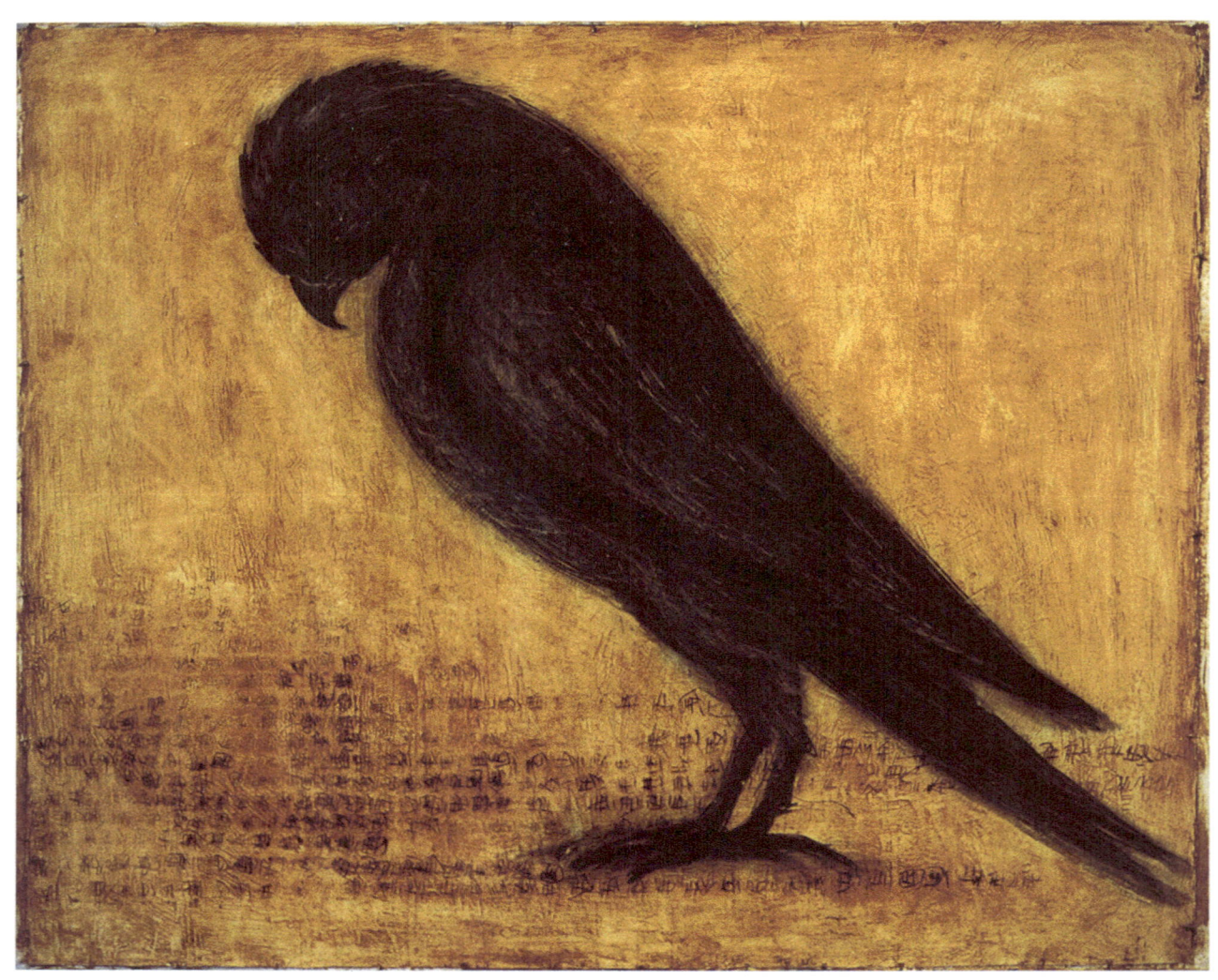

How to be a bird, oil, wax, on primed paper   1996

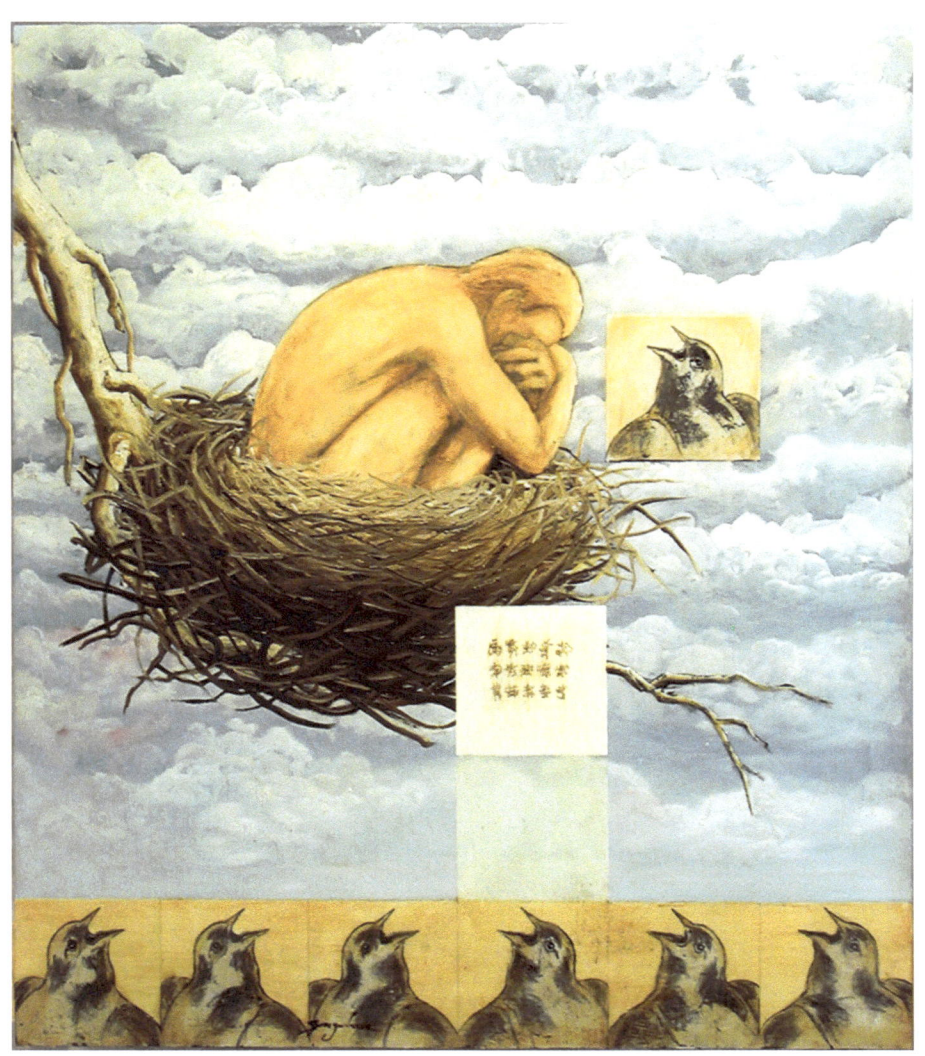

Intruder, oil, wax, on panel   2009

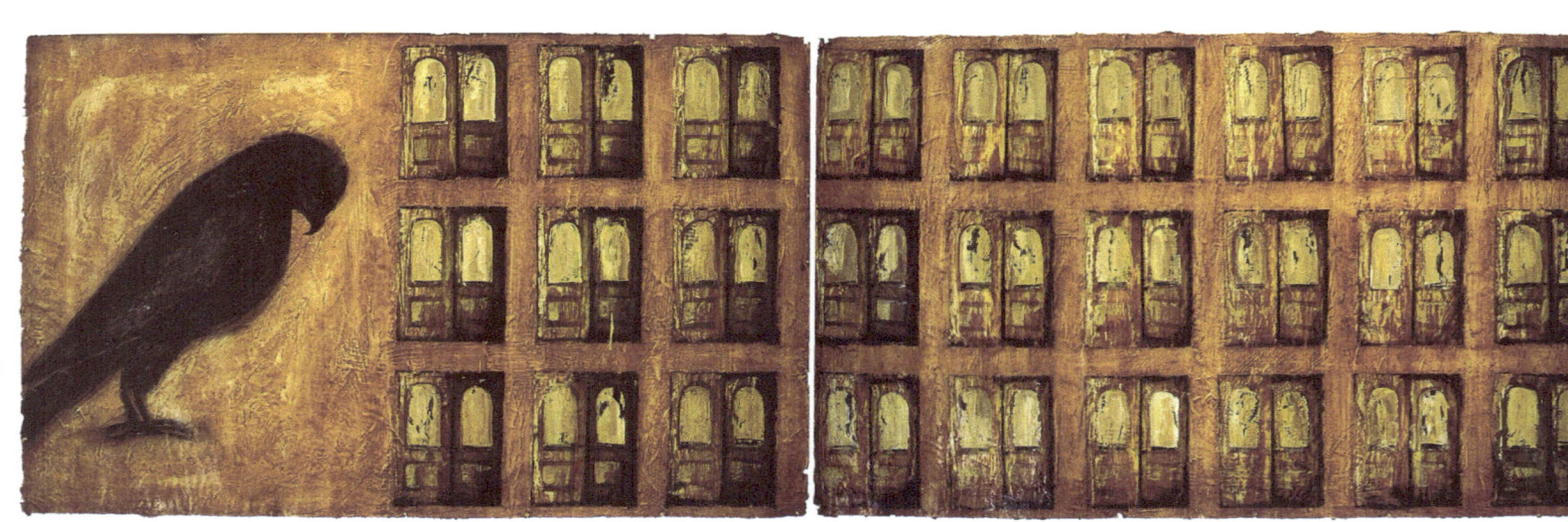

Knocking on doors, oil, wax, on primed paper   1996

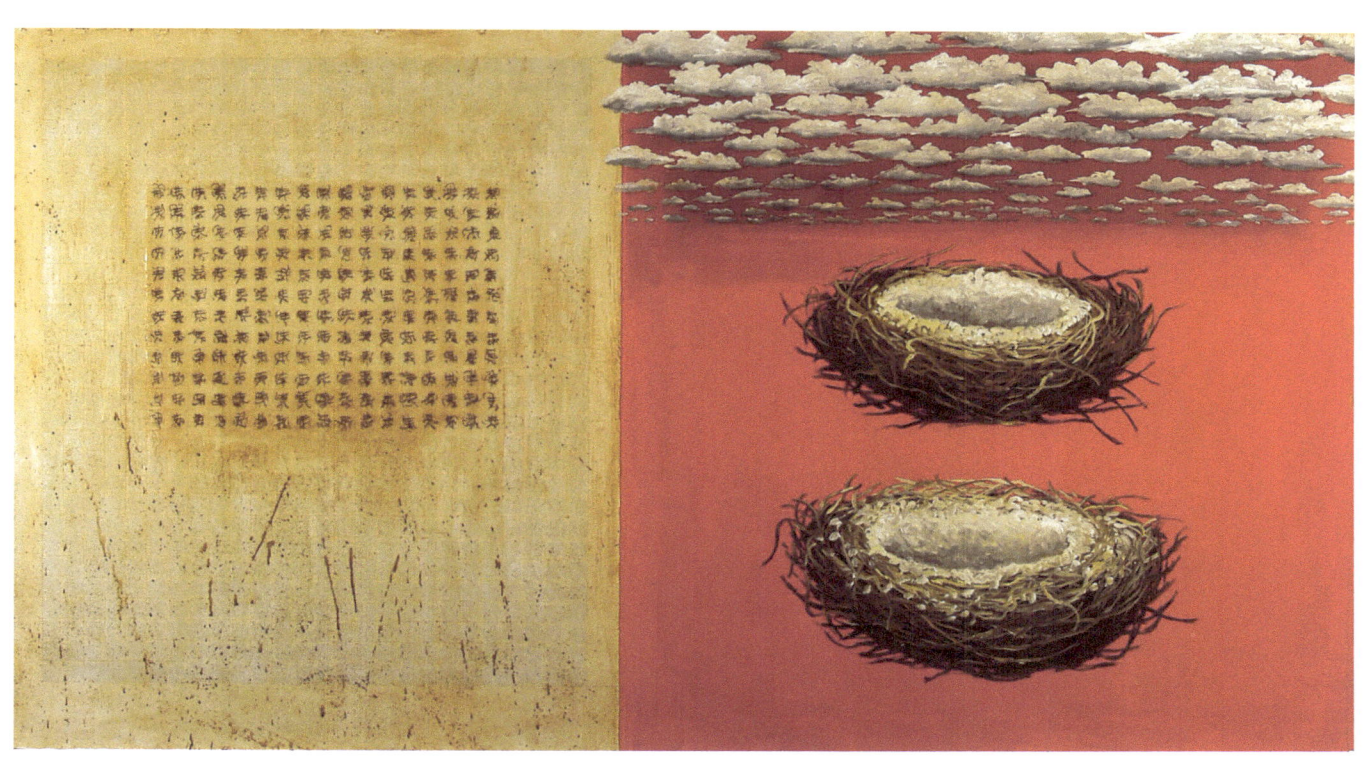

Life, oil, wax, on primed paper   2002

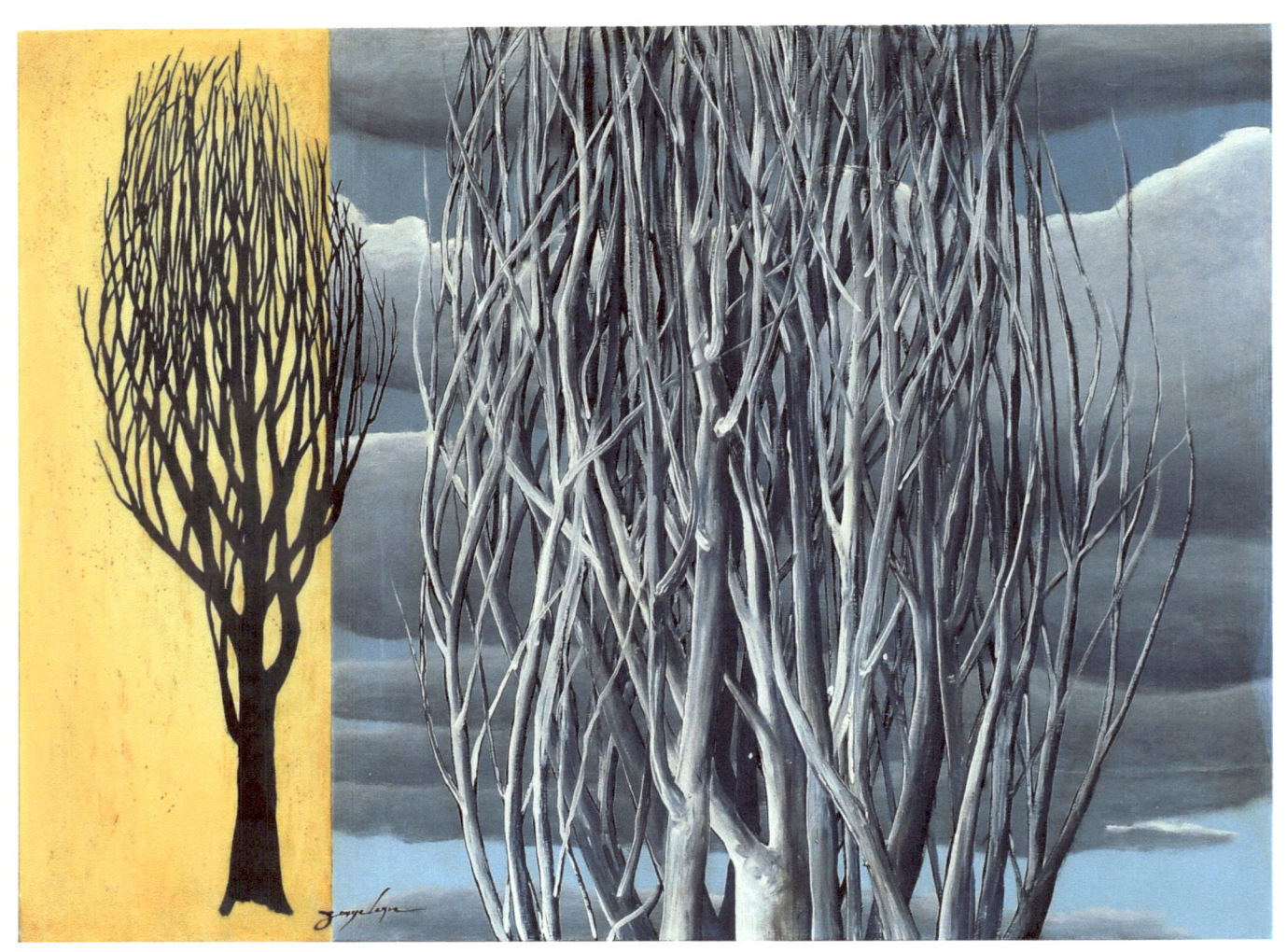

Nest Tree, oil, wax, on canvas   2008

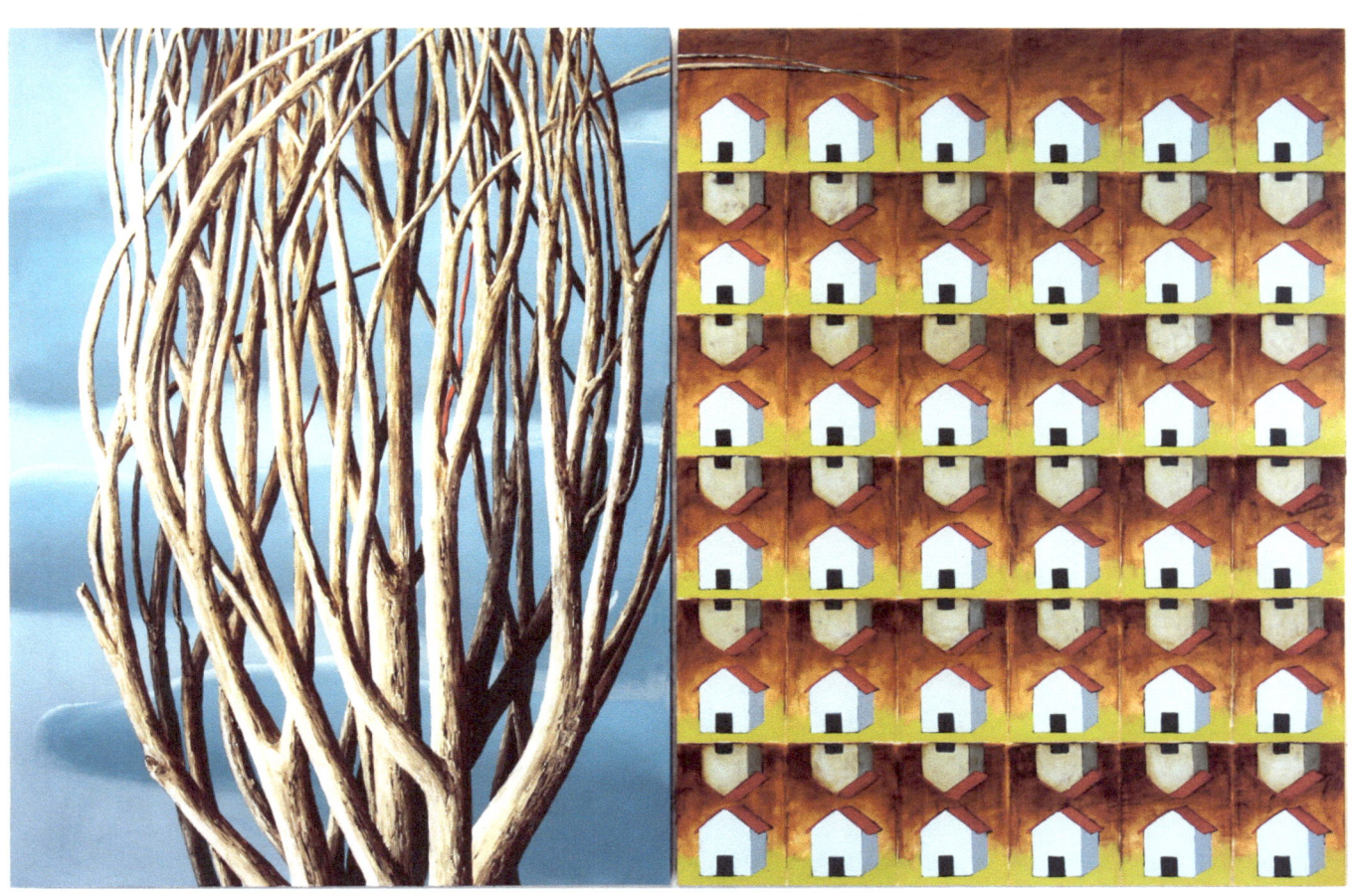

Red Creek Branch, oil on panel   2012

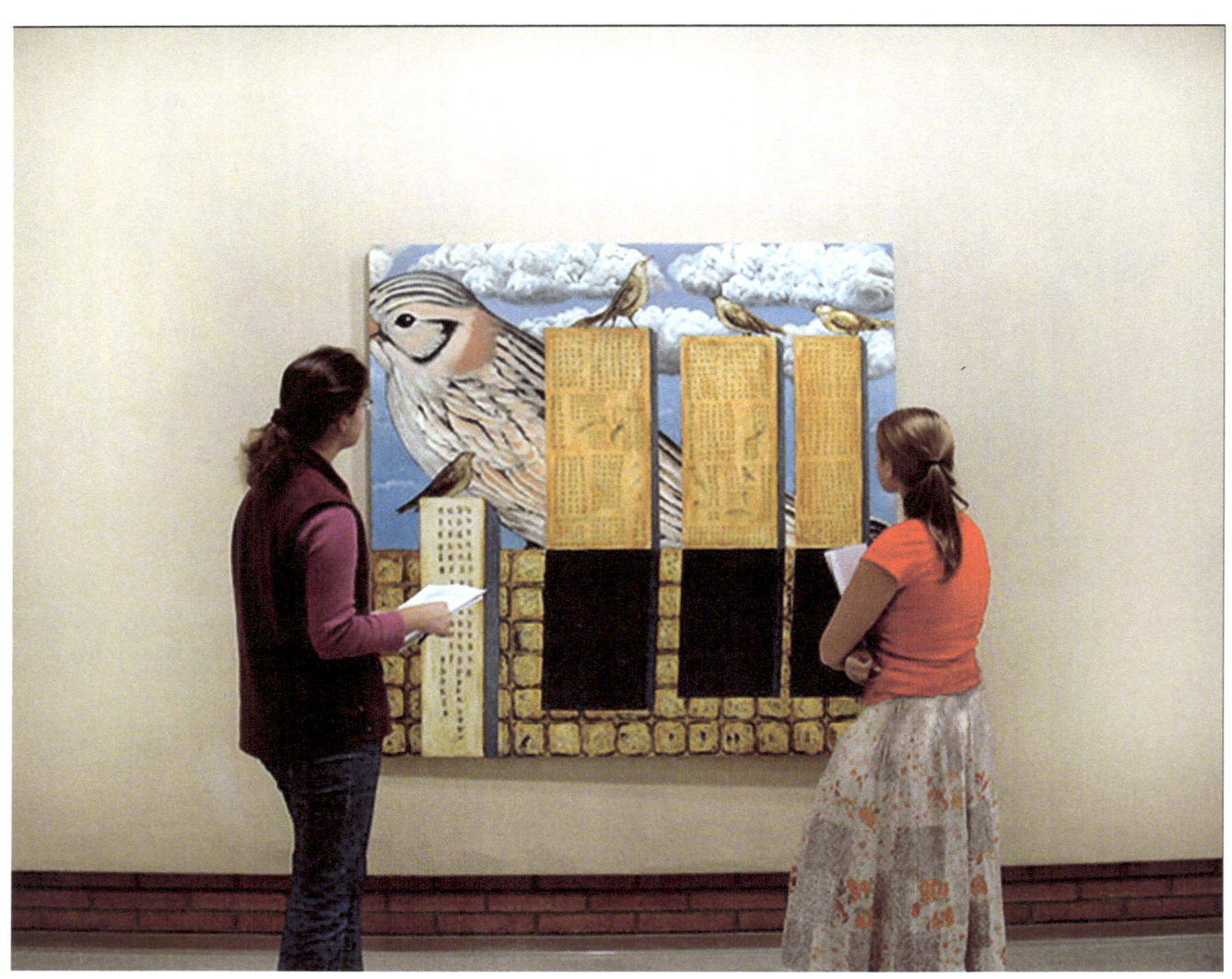

Skyscraper Birds, oil, on canvas over wood 2006

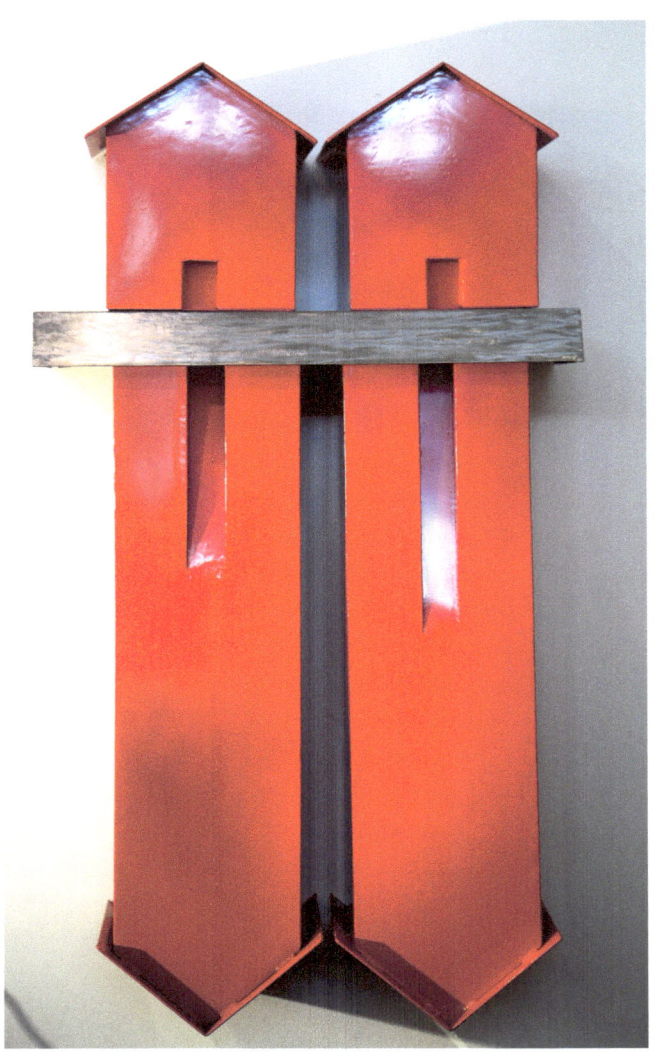
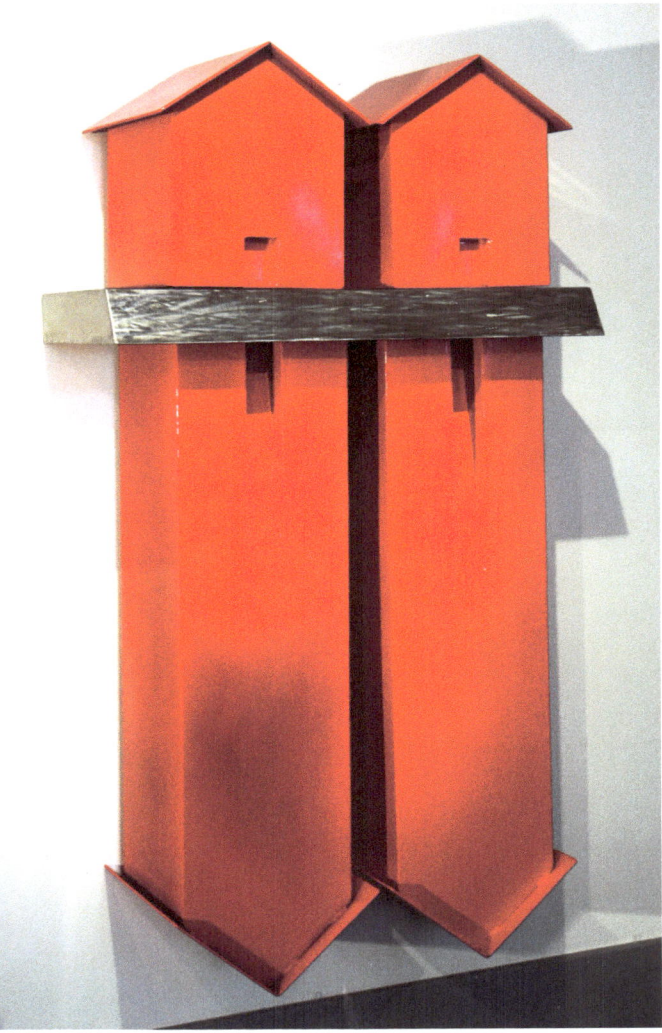

Sunset at silver lake, powdered coated steel, stainless steel   2013

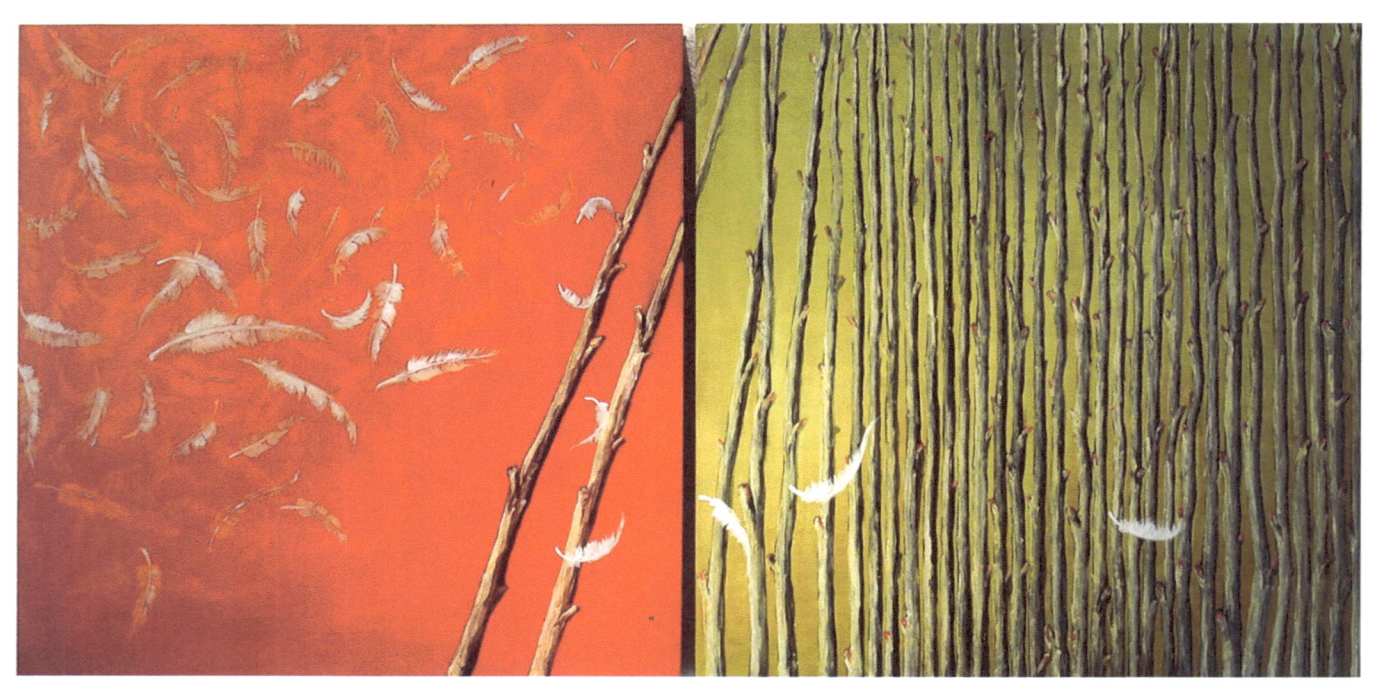

The Air, oil on panel   2012

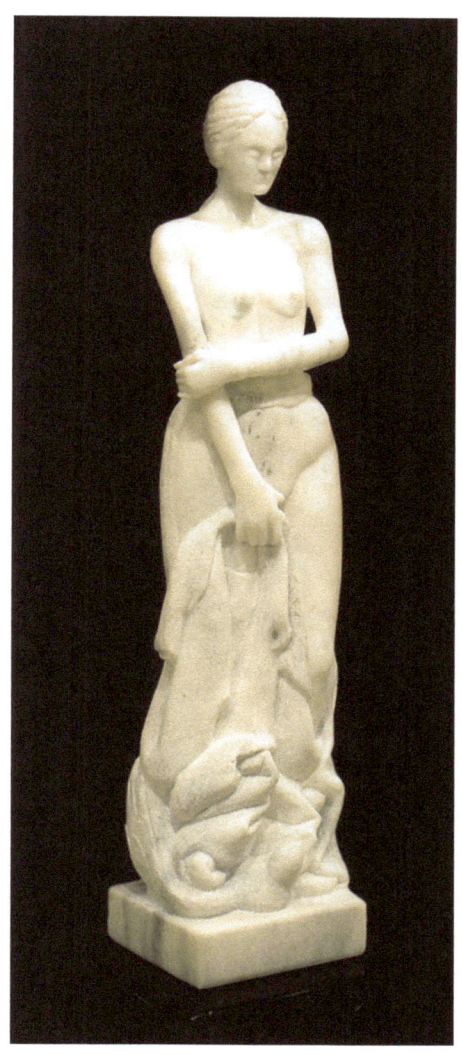

The Bird Handler, marble   2008

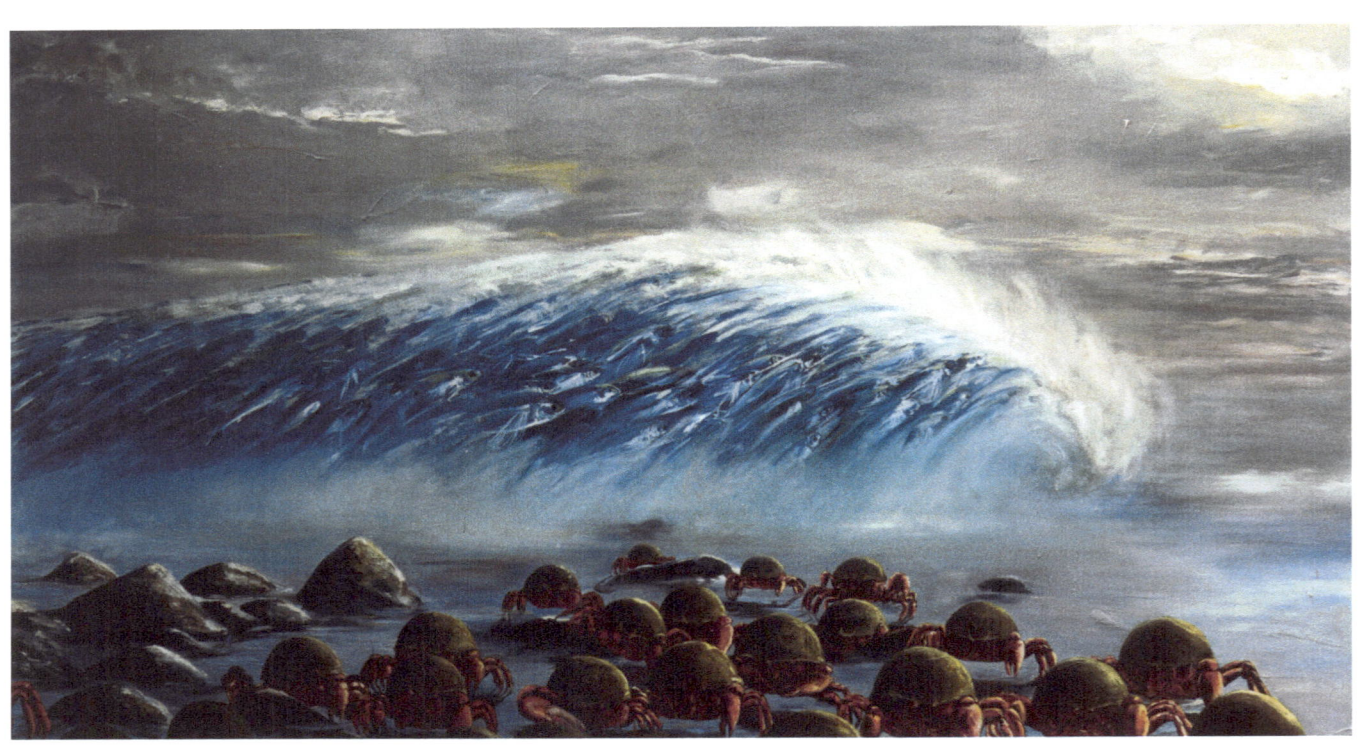

The Dawning Coast, oil, on canvas   1995

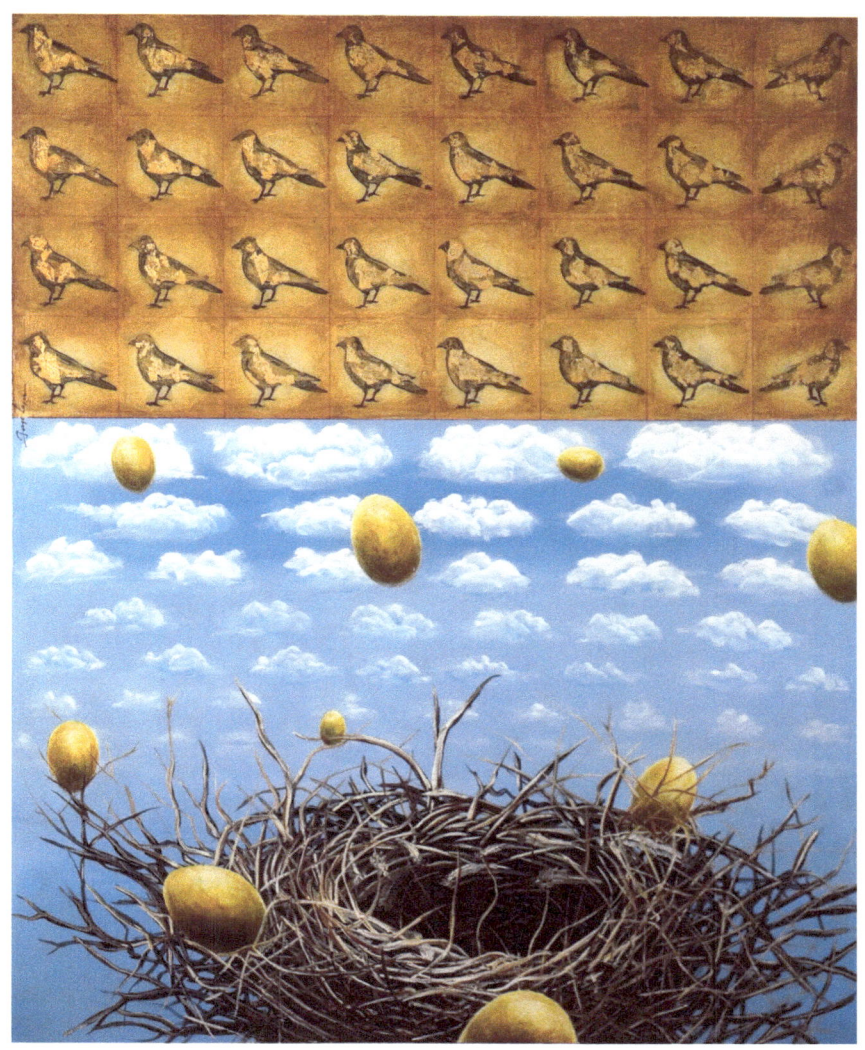

The Golden Eggs, oil, on panel 2004

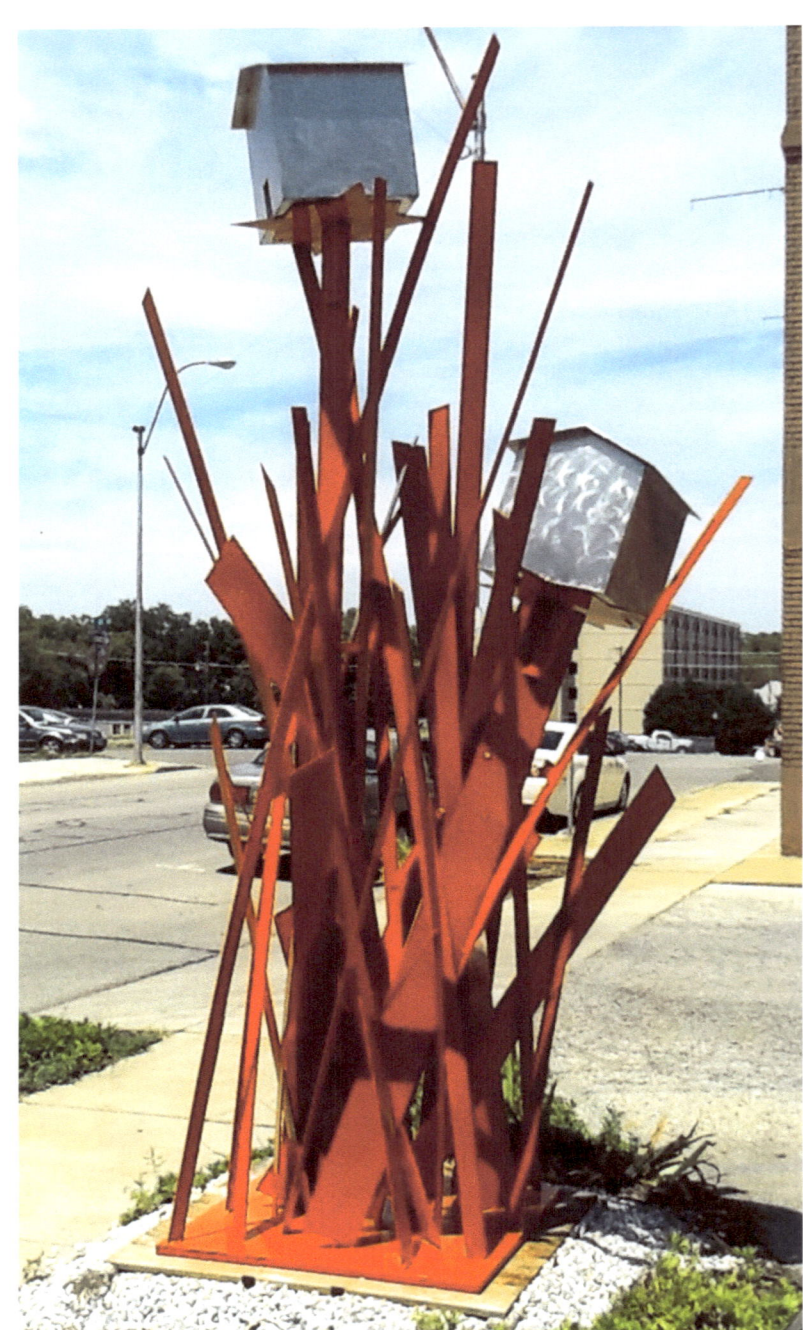

The reeds in red and
silver, powder coated
steel, stainless steel 2013

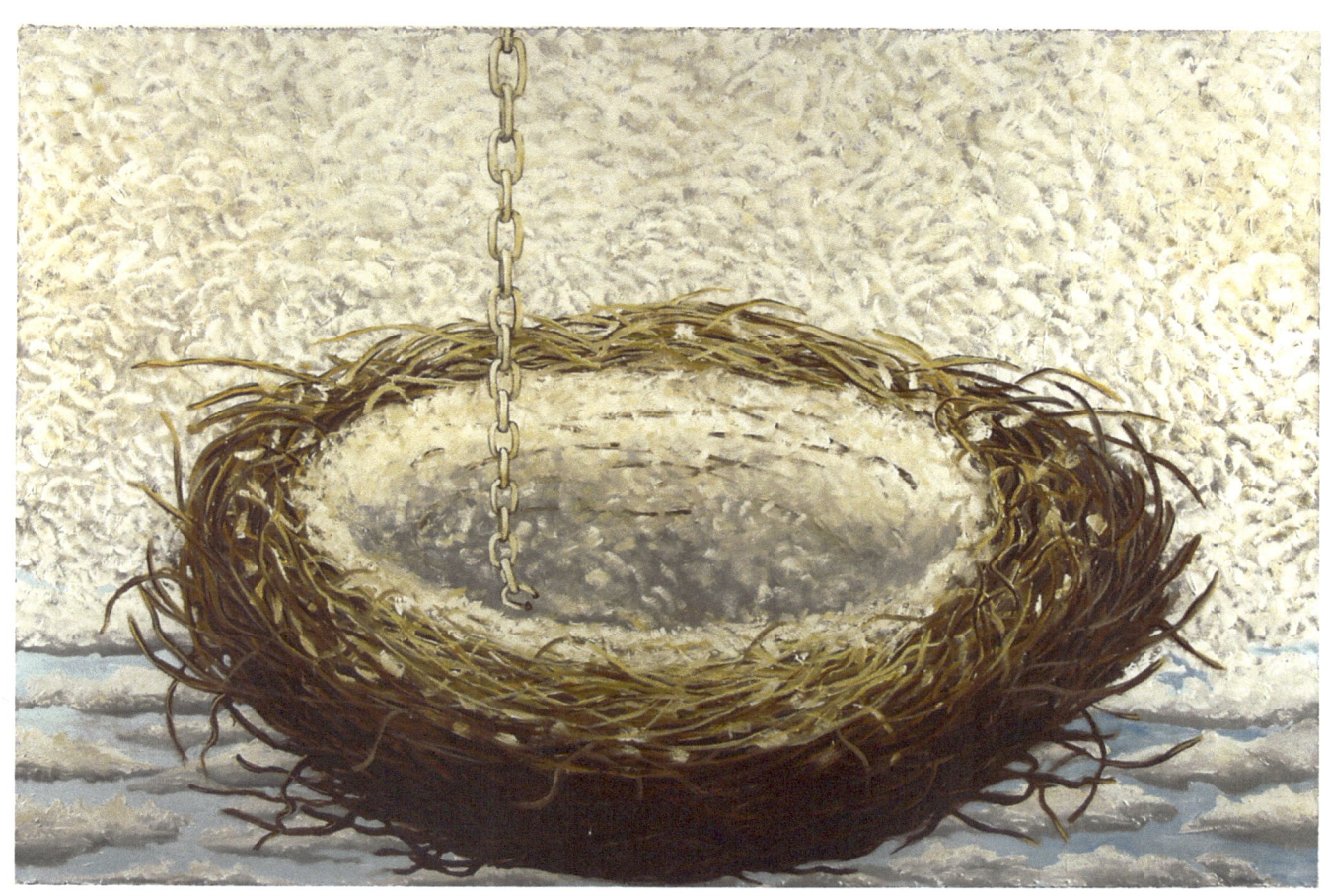

The Scape, oil, on primed paper   1998

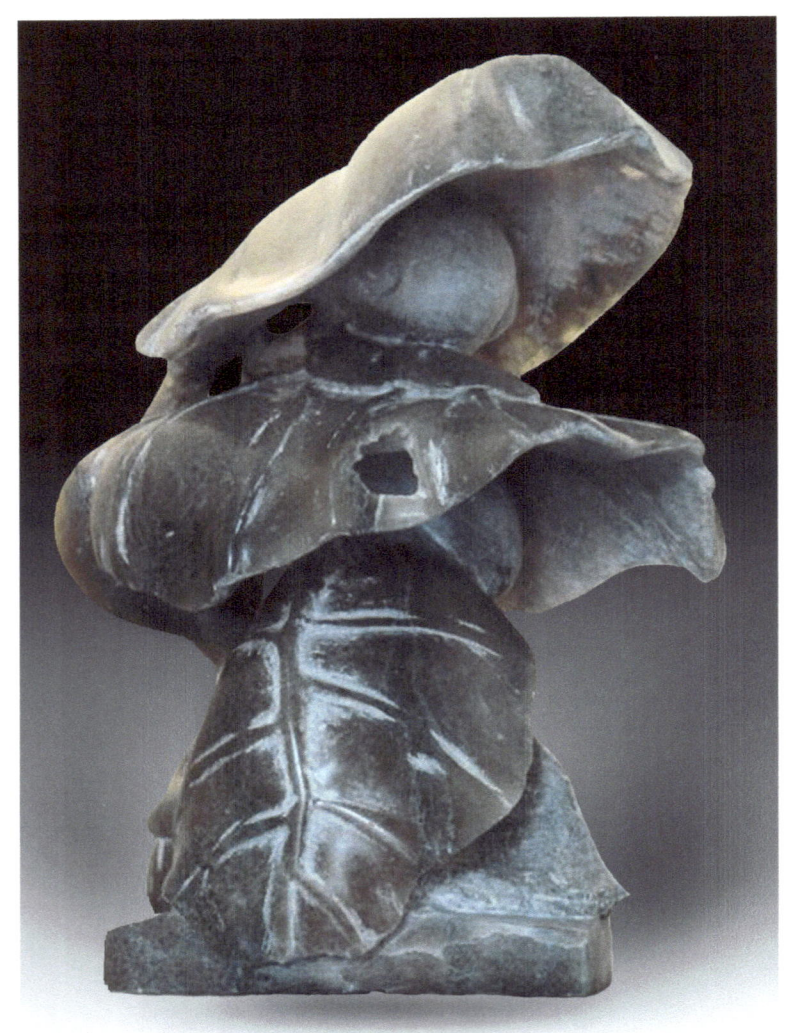

The Snail, alabaster   2004

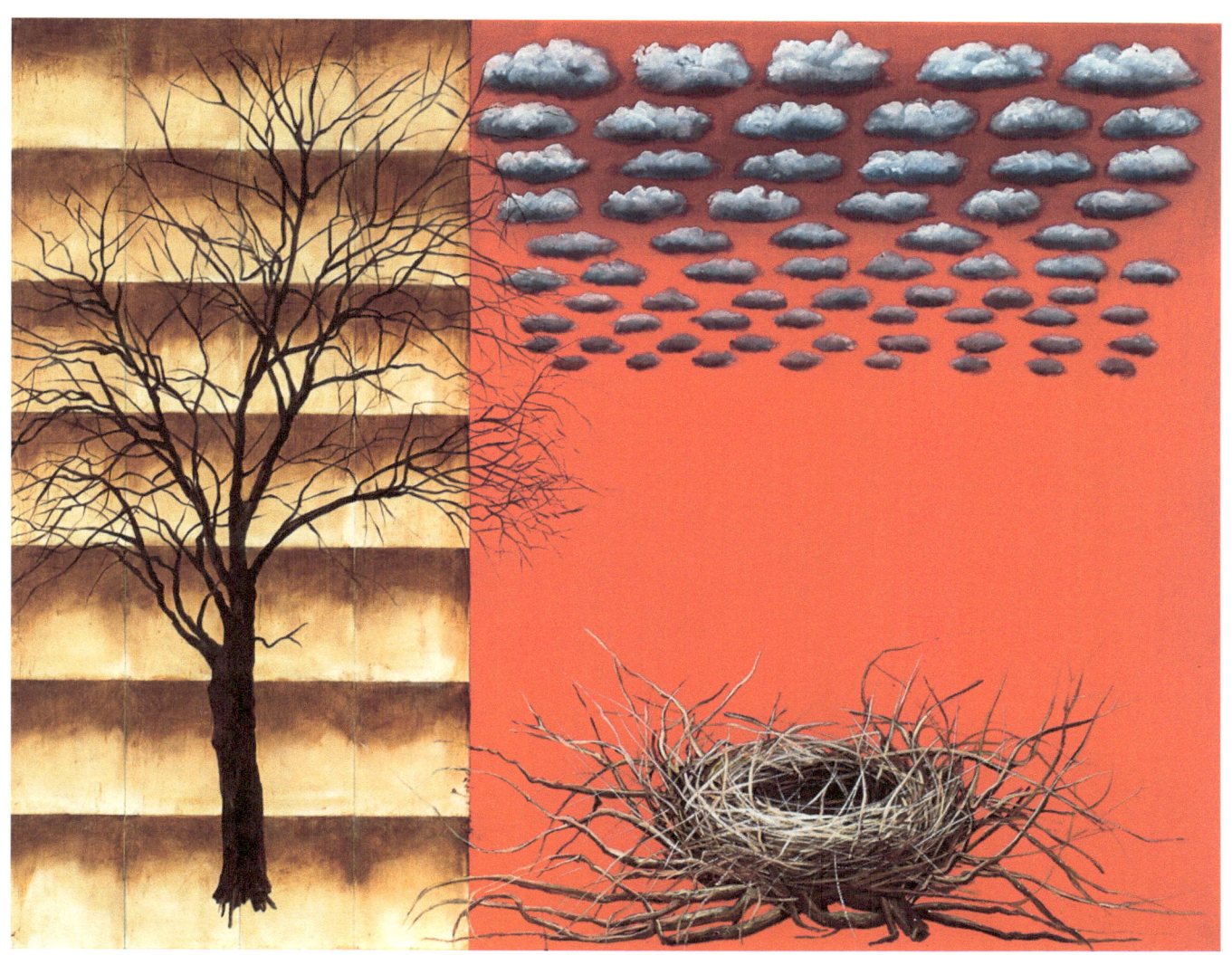

The Wind, oil, wax, on panel   2007

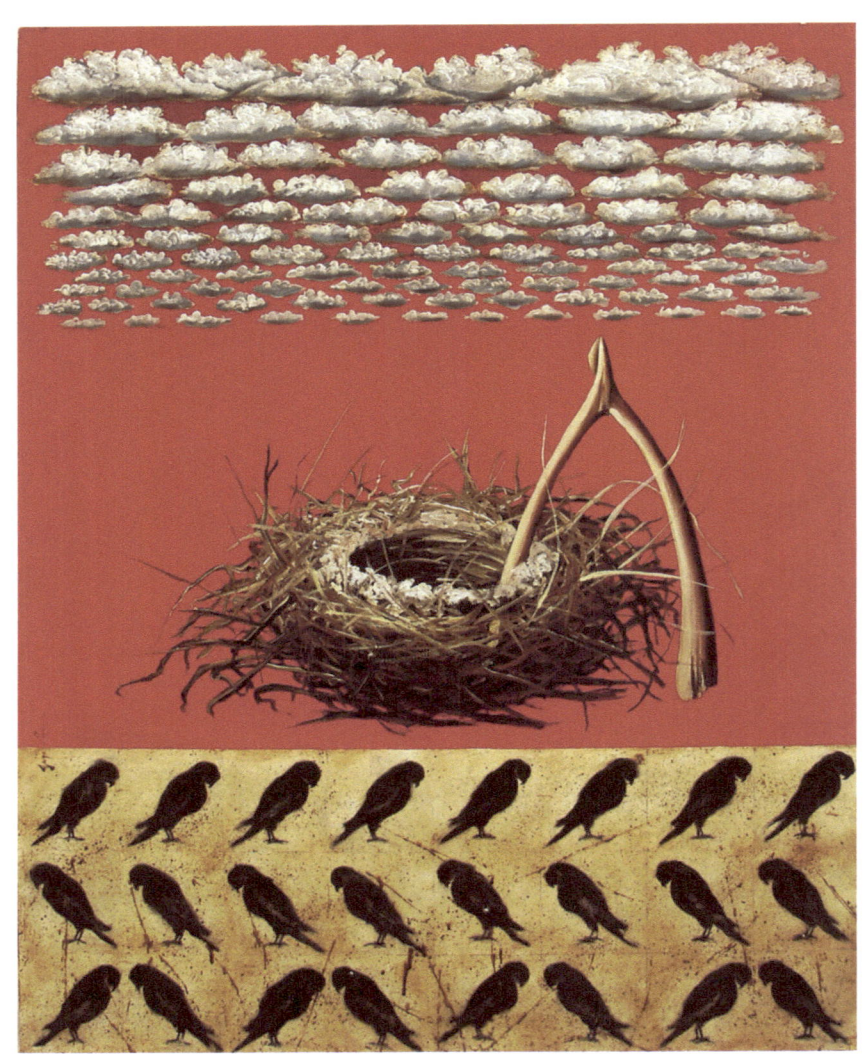

The Wish, oil, wax, on primed paper 2004

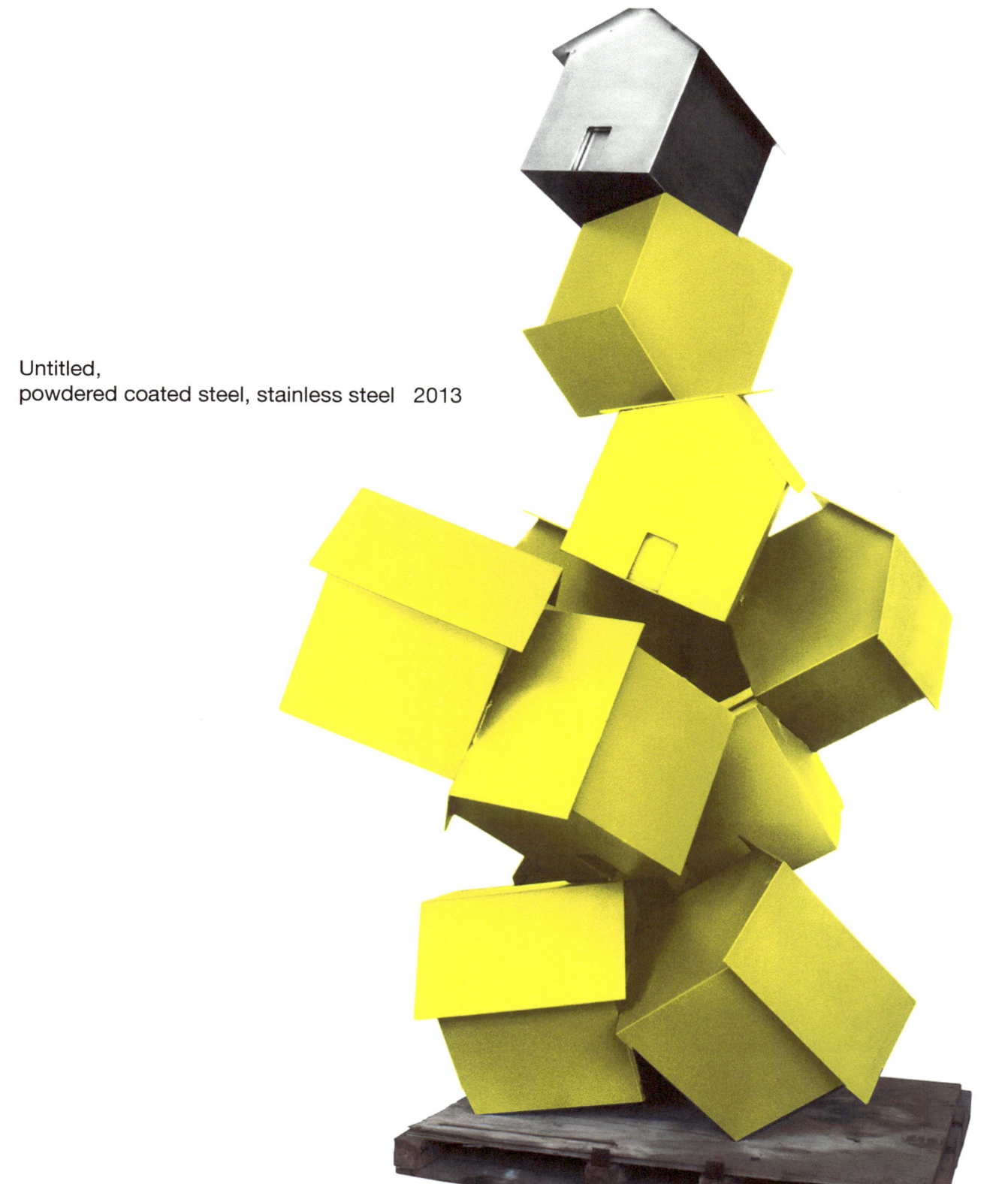

Untitled,
powdered coated steel, stainless steel   2013

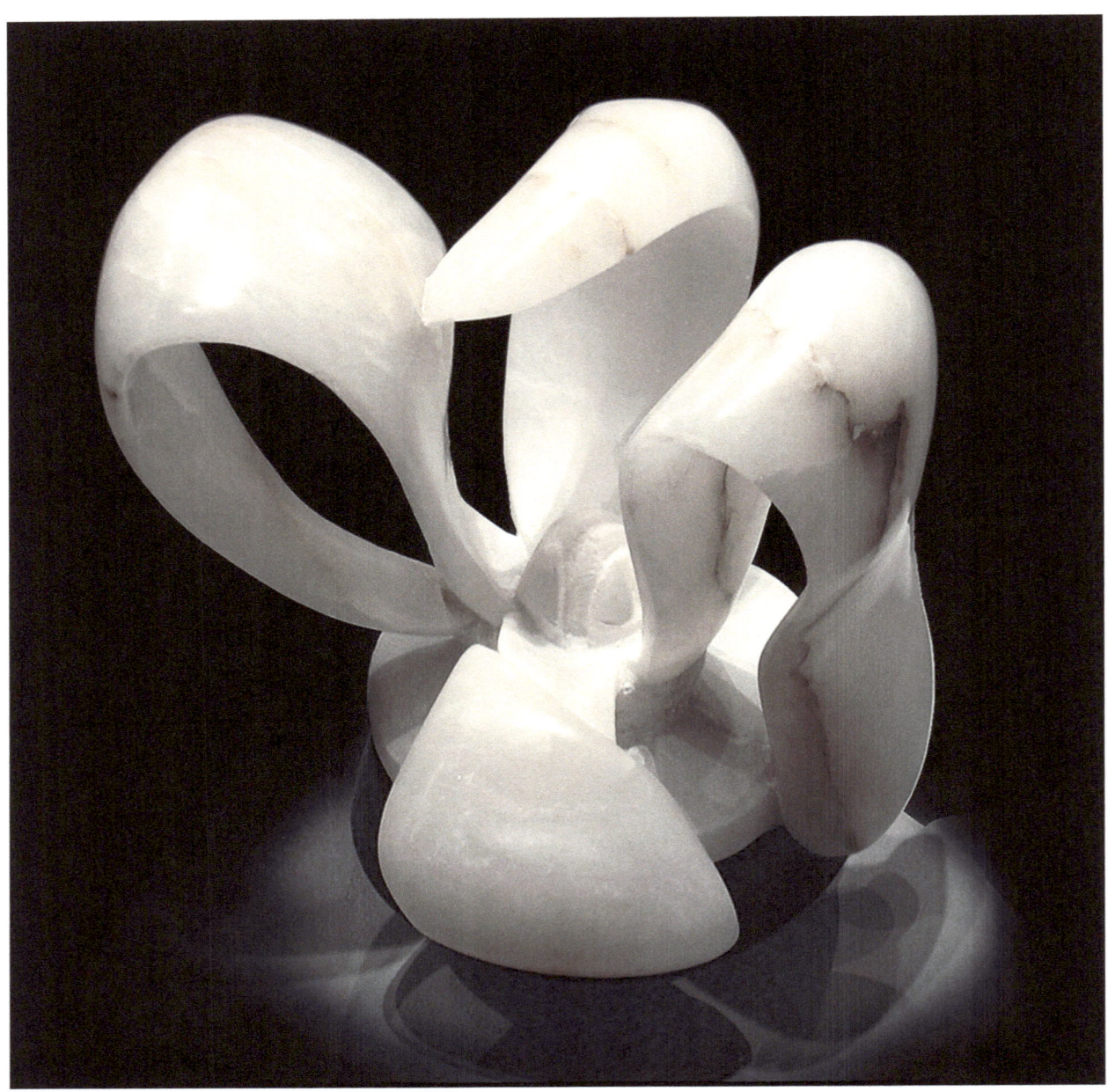

White Cactus, italian ice alabaster   2003

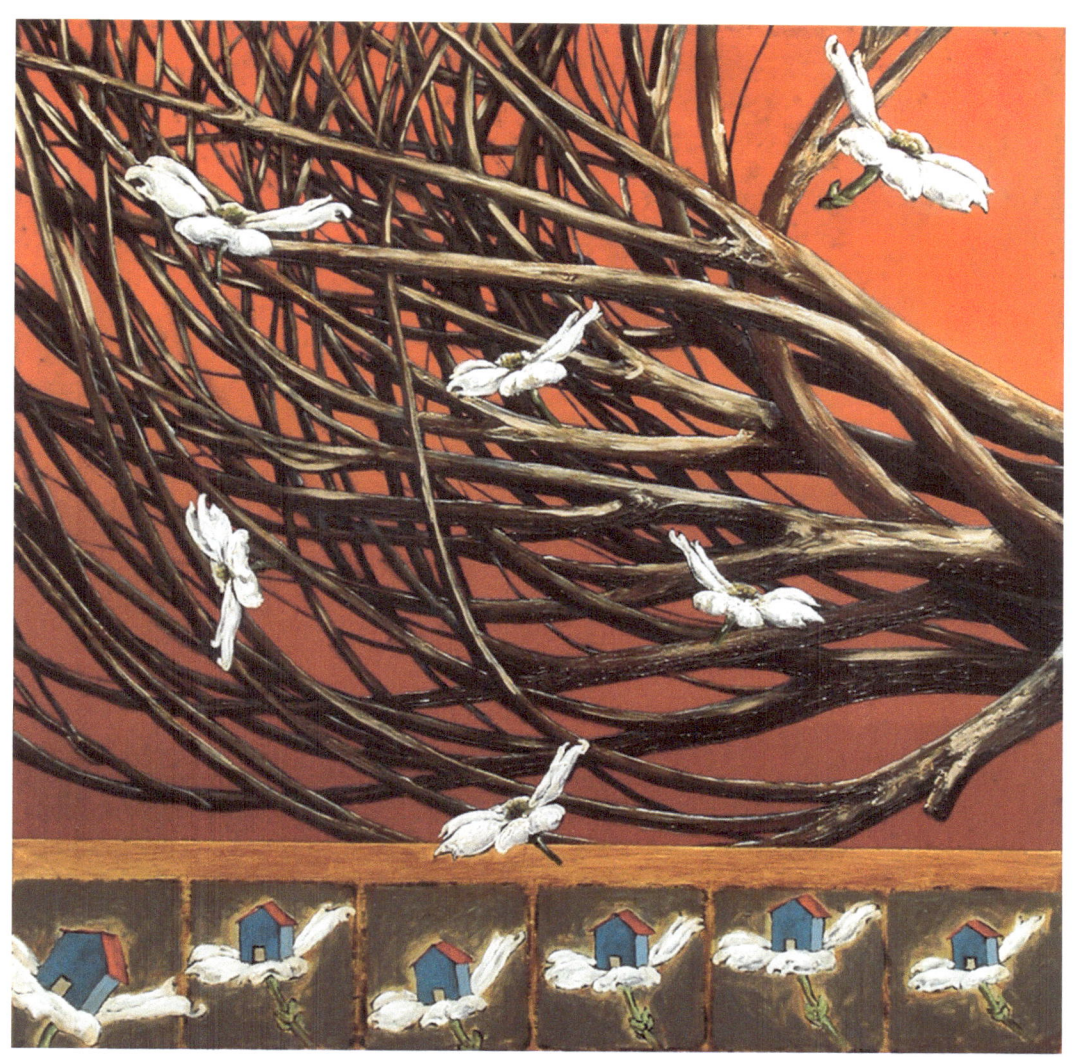

Wind riders scape, oil, on panel   2010

This book is dedicated by the Artist

To my mentor, friend and patron, Peggy Koehler

Who I am as an artist was not achieved alone by hard work and talent. Many people throughout my lifetime have played an important role in helping me get here. Teachers, friends, family, supporters and collectors. Though every one of these people are worthy of mentioning by name, no one is more worthy than Peggy Koehler. She is quite an amazing woman, with whom I have spent thirty of my fifty five years of life. She saw an artist, and she pulled it out of me, with her courage, her generosity her love and her persistence. To her I dedicate my career in the arts and this book of my paintings and sculptures.

Jorge Leyva

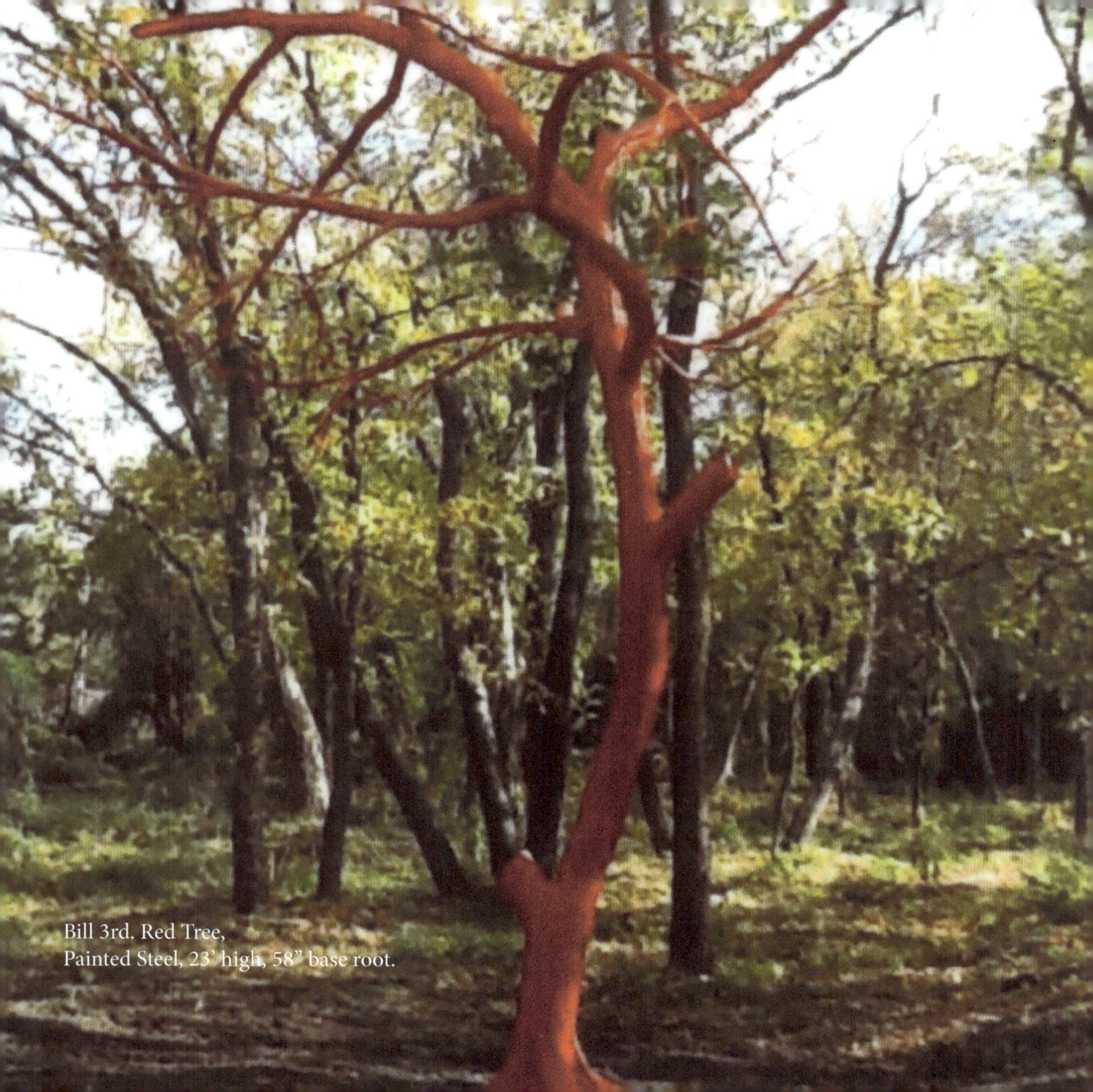

Bill 3rd. Red Tree,
Painted Steel, 23' high, 58" base root.

www.ingramcontent.com/pod-product-compliance
Lightning Source LLC
Chambersburg PA
CBHW050403180526
45159CB00005B/2127